The Gig Bag Book of
GUITAR TAB
CHORDS

Over 2100+ chords for all guitarists presented in a unique tablature system.

Compiled by Mark Bridges

EXCLUSIVELY DISTRIBUTED BY
HAL•LEONARD®

Order No. AM943250
ISBN 978-07119-6489-1
This book © Copyright 2007 by Wise Publications.

Interior design and layout: Mark Bridges.

Contents

Introduction

This book is a reference guide for guitarists. It is not intended as a method book, but rather as a reference book of chords that are easily accessible to the beginner or advanced guitarist. Regardless of your musical interest, this book contains the majority of chords you will encounter in most styles of music (rock, jazz, country, or blues). Strong chord knowledge will help build familiarity with the fretboard and help develop flexibility in solo, accompaniment or ensemble playing.

The forty-two chord types covered in this book are:

• major	• 7
• 6	• 9
• $\frac{6}{9}$	• 13
• maj7	• 7♭9
• maj13	• 7♯9
• maj9	• 7+
• maj9♯11	• 7♭9
• maj7+	• 7♭5
• maj7♭5	• 7$^{\sharp 9}_{\flat 5}$
• maj13(no9)	• 7$^{\sharp 9}_{\sharp 5}$
• add9	• 9♯11
• minor	• 9+
• m7	• 7sus4
• m6	• 9sus4
• m(maj7)	• 13sus4
• m(add9)	• o
• m9	• m7♭5
• m(maj9)	• o7
• m$\frac{6}{9}$	• +
• m11(no9)	• sus4
• m11	• sus2

In addition to these chord types, this book also contains special sections on Powerchords and Slash Chords further adding to the completeness of this collection. Although there are many more chord types available, these chord types were chosen for their popularity as well as their usefulness.

The Gig Bag Book of GuitarTab Chords has been designed with the player in mind. You don't have to go to your bookshelf to find that bulky chord encyclopedia that your music stand can't even hold up, you don't have to break the spine of the book to get it to stay open, and it doesn't take up all the space on your music stand. It is easy-to-carry and easy-to-use. We hope that this book will serve as a valuable reference source during your years as a developing guitarist.

How to Use this Book

It is strongly recommended that you develop a practice regimen in which you devote some time to chord study. If you practice one hour each session, then devote fifteen or twenty minutes to chord study. Another approach would be to practice your warm-up exercises with a different chord type each day.

Here are some helpful tips:

• Above each chord grid you will find the name of the chord and to the right you'll find the chord spelled out on the treble staff.
• Each chord type has several variations that extend the length of the fretboard. Each variation is presented from the lowest position on the neck to the highest position on the neck.
• Use the following legend to construct the desired chord.

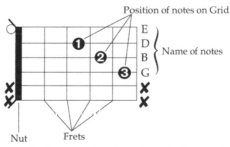

Whether you are looking to develop *chops* (technique) or broaden your chord vocabulary, *The Gig Bag Book of GuitarTab Chords* is for you.

C

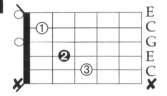

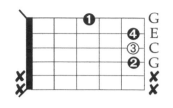

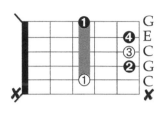

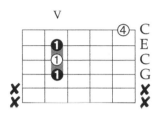

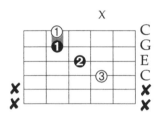

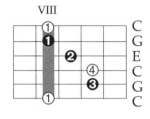

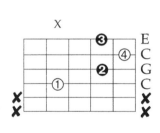

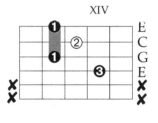

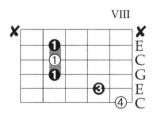

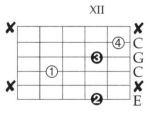

C6

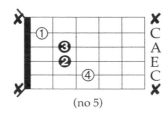
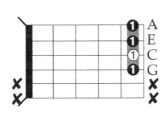

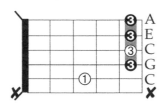

(no 5)

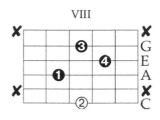
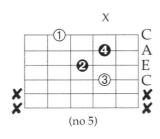

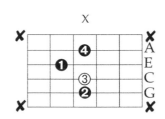

(no 5)

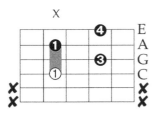

C $^6_9$

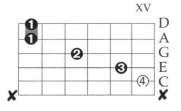

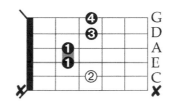
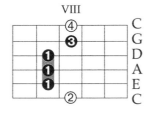

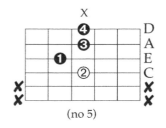

(no 5)

C

Cmaj7

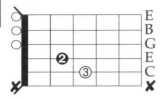

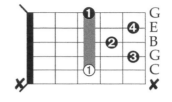

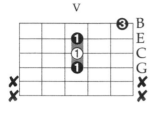

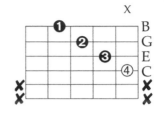

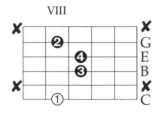

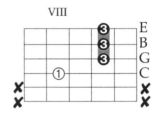

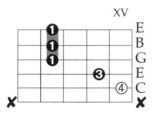

Cmaj13

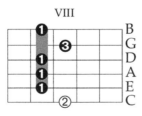

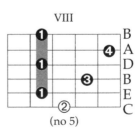

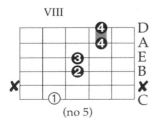

Cmaj9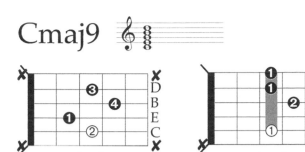

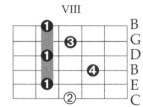

(no 5)

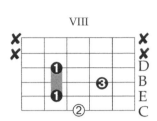

(no 3)

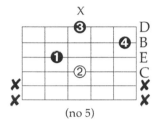

(no 5)

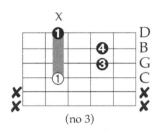

(no 3)

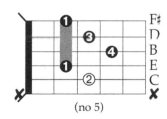

(no 5)

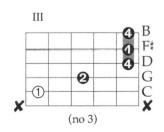

(no 3)

Cmaj9#11

(no 5)

(no 3)

(no 5)

C

Cmaj7+

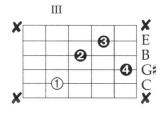
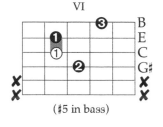

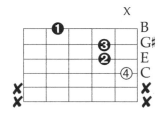
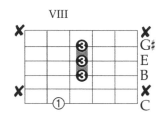

(♯5 in bass)

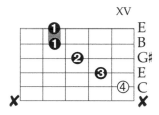

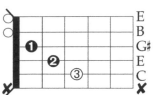

Cmaj7♭5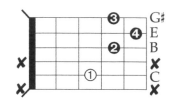

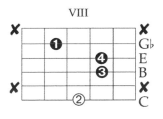
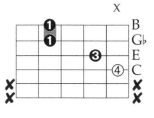

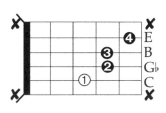
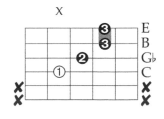

Cmaj13(no9)

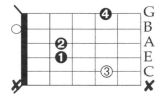

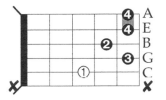

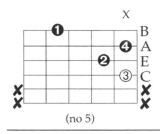

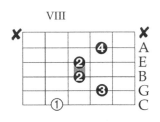

(no 5)

Cadd9

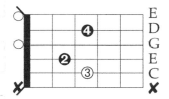

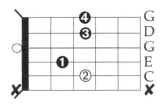

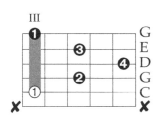

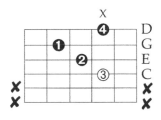

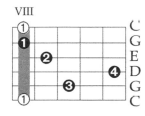

Cm

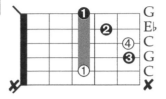

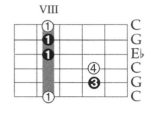

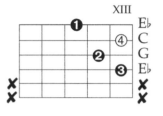

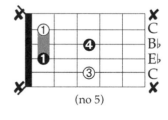

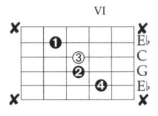

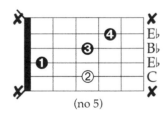

Cm7

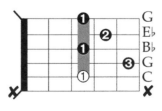

(no 5)   (no 5)

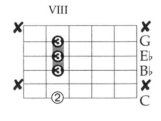

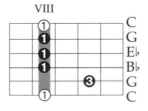

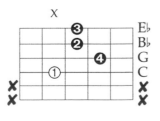

Cm6

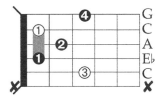
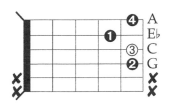
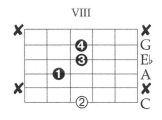
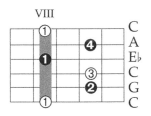
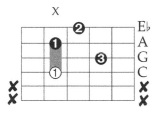

Cm(maj7)

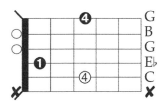
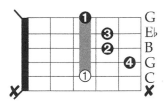
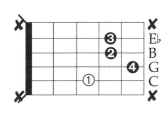
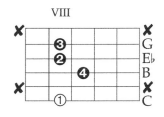
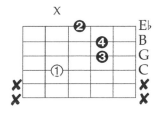
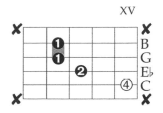

C

C

Cm add9

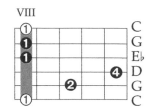

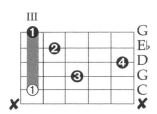

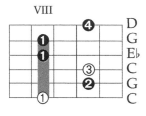

Cm9

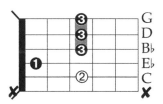

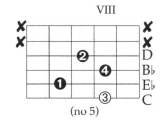

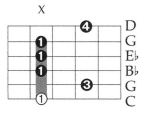

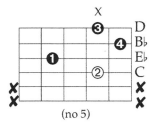

Cm(maj9)

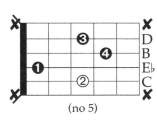

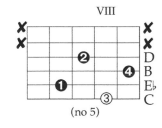

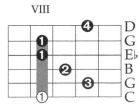

Cm⁶₉

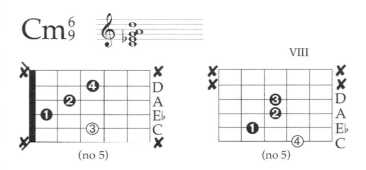

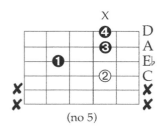
(no 5)

VIII
(no 5)

X
(no 5)

VIII

Cm11(no9)

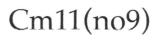

G
E♭
B♭
F
C

X
(no 5)

VIII
(no 5)

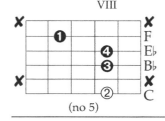

Cm11

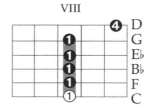

VIII

D
G
E♭
B♭
F
C

C7

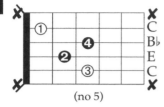 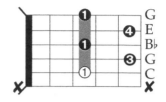

(no 5)

III   V

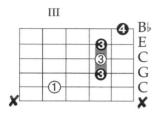 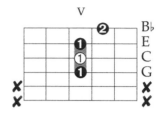

VIII   X

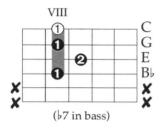 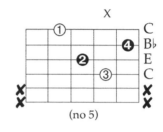

(♭7 in bass)   (no 5)

VIII   VIII

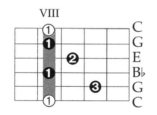 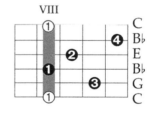

X   XIV

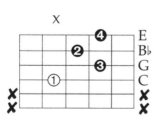 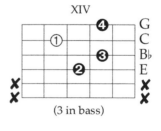

(3 in bass)

C9

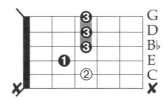

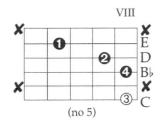

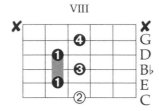

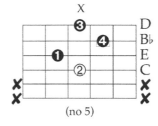

C13

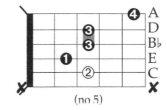

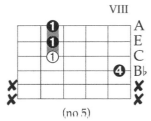

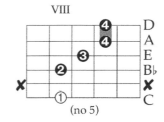

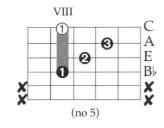

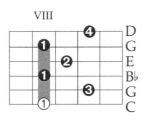

C

C7♭9

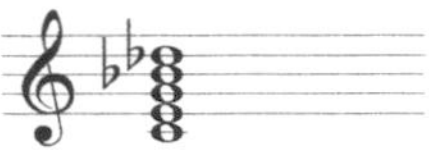

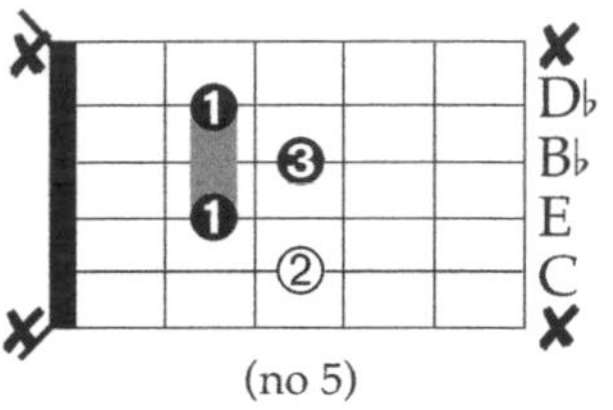

(no 5)

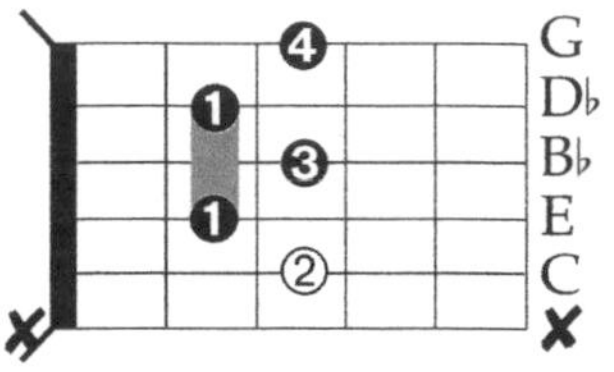

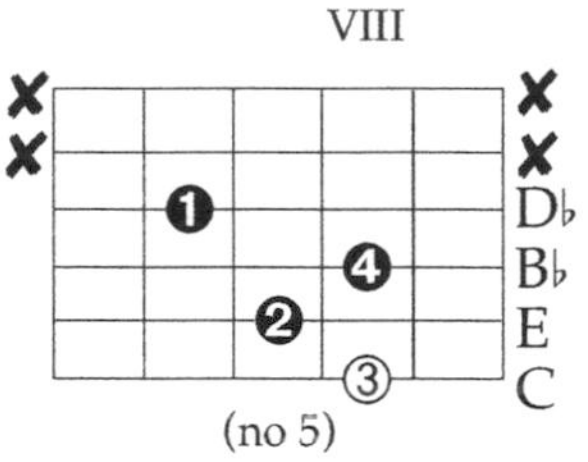

(no 5)

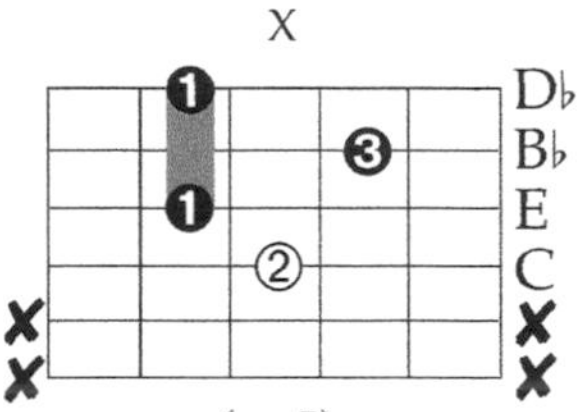

(no 5)

C7♯9

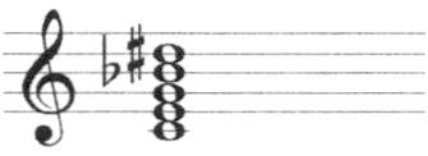

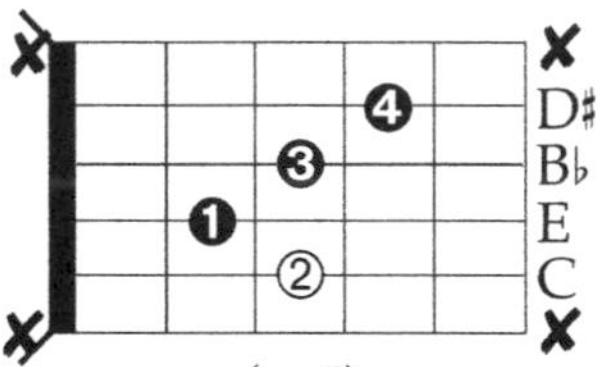

(no 5)

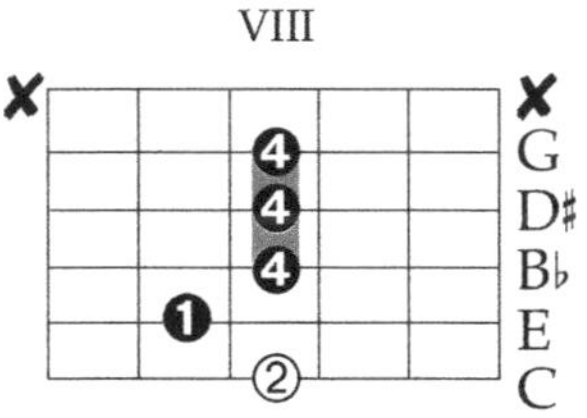

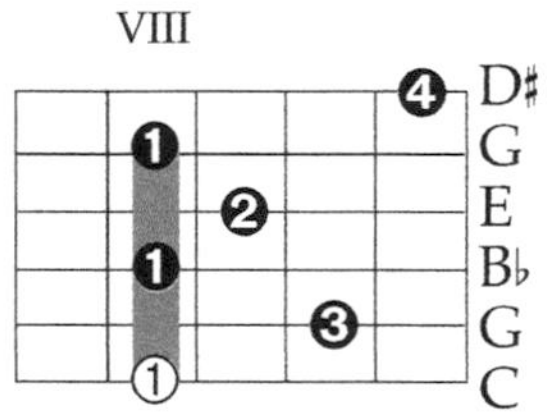

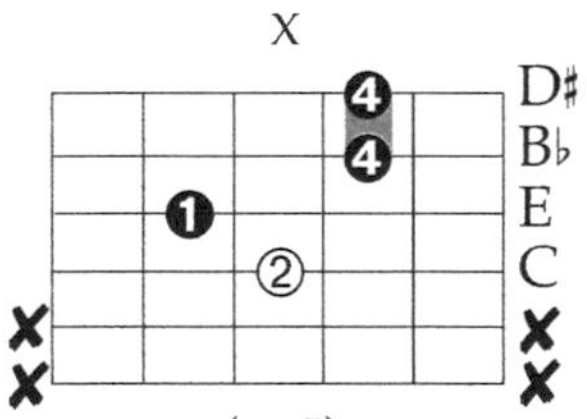

(no 5)

C13♭9

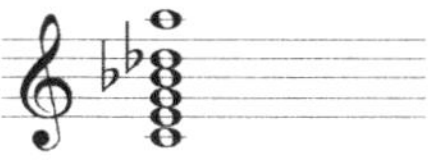

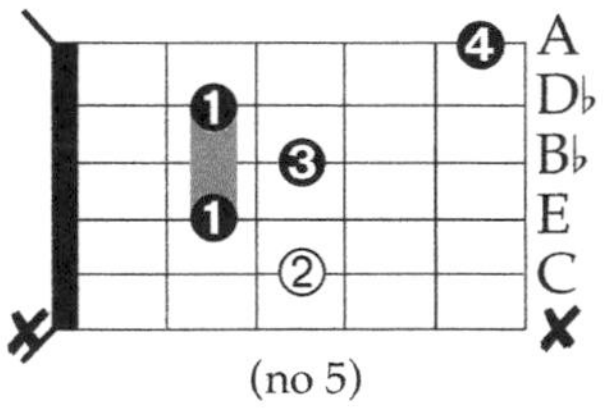

(no 5)

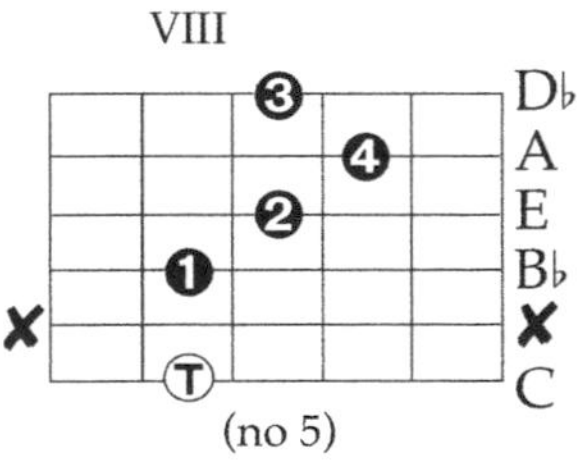

(no 5)

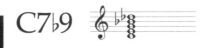

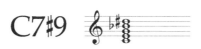

C7+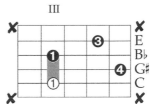

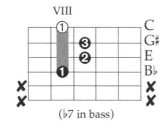

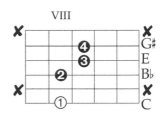

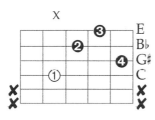

(♭7 in bass)

C7♭5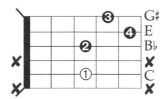

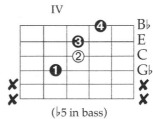

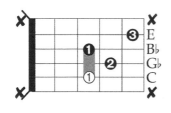

(♭5 in bass)

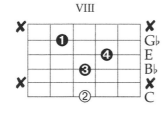

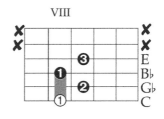

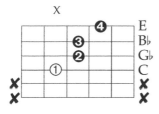

C

C

C7$^{\flat9}_{\sharp5}$

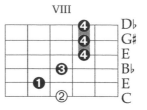

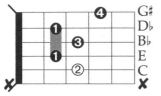

C7$^{\sharp9}_{\sharp5}$

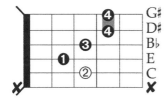

C9♯11

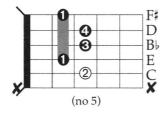

(no 5)   (no 5)

C9+

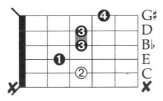
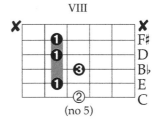
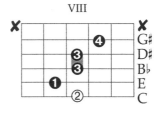
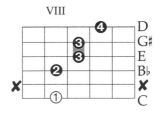

C7sus4

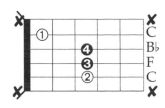
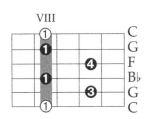

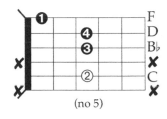
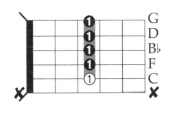

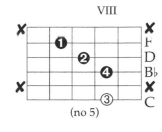

C9sus4

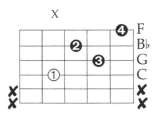
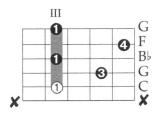

(no 5)

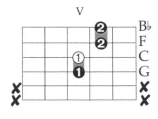
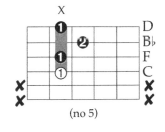

(no 5)   (no 5)

C13sus4

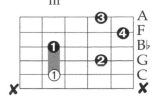
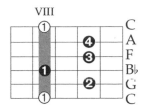

C

C°

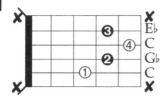
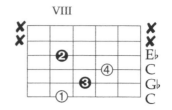

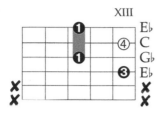

Cm7♭5

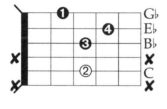
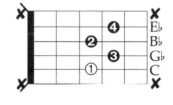

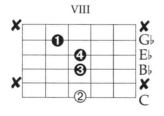
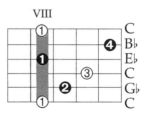

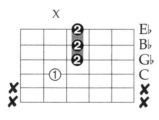

C°7

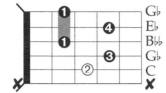

Gb
Eb
Bbb
Gb
C

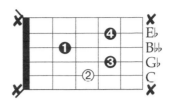

Eb
Bbb
Gb
C

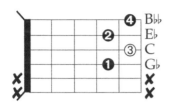

Bbb
Eb
C
Gb

VII

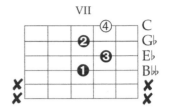

C
Gb
Eb
Bbb

VIII

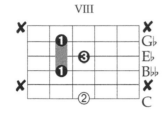

Gb
Eb
Bbb
C

VIII

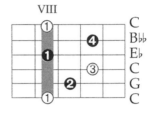

C
Bbb
Eb
C
G
C

X

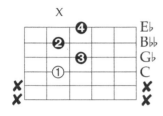

Eb
Bbb
Gb
C

C

C+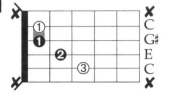

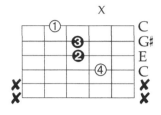

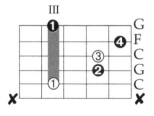

Csus4

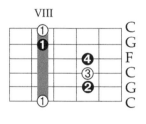

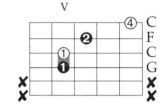

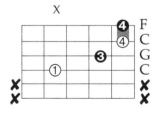

Csus2

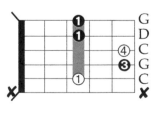

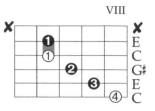

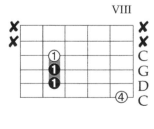

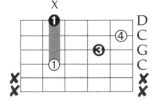

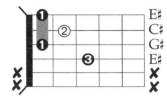

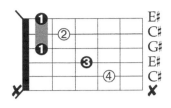

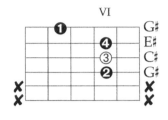

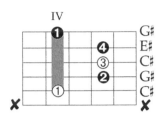

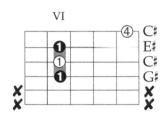

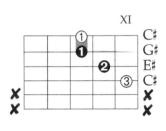

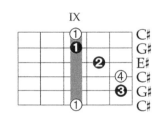

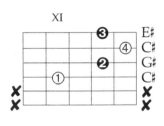

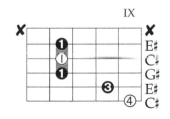

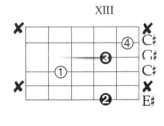

C#6

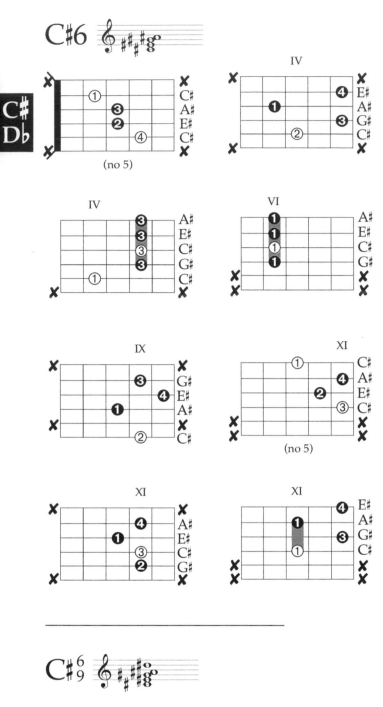

(no 5)

IV

IV

VI

IX

XI

(no 5)

XI

XI

C#⁶₉

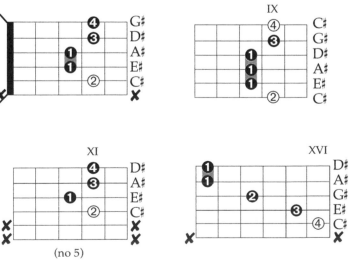

IX

XI

(no 5)

XVI

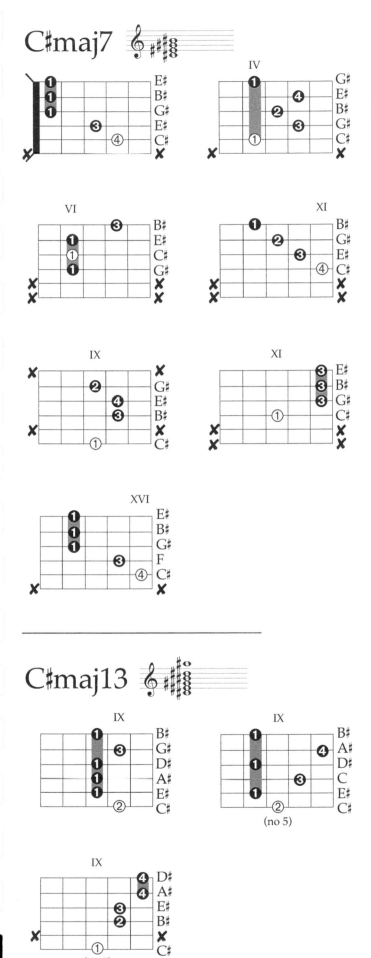

C#maj7

C#
Db

C#maj13

C#maj9

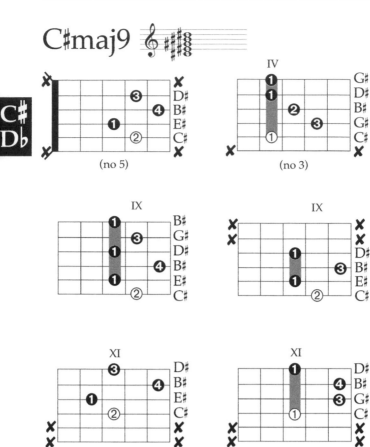

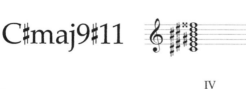

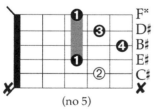

C#maj9#11

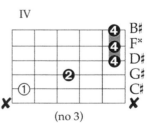

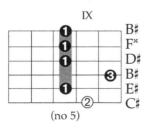

C#maj7+

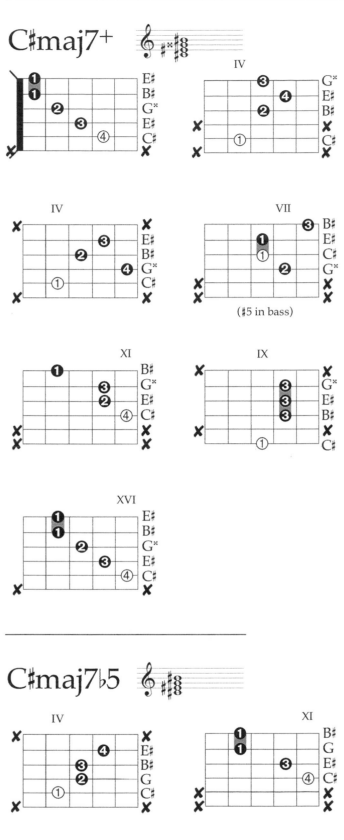

(#5 in bass)

C#maj7♭5

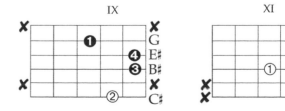

C#maj13(no9)

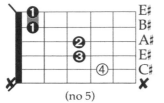
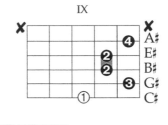

(no 5)

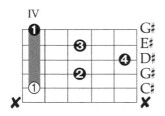
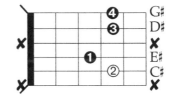

(no 5)

C#add9

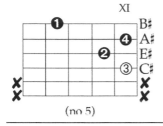
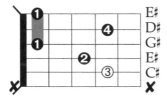

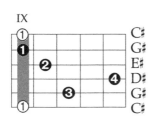
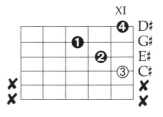

C#m

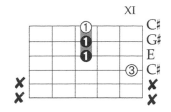

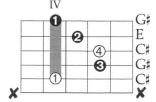
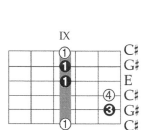

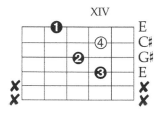
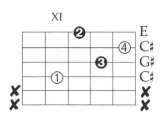

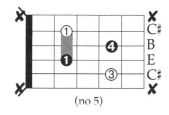
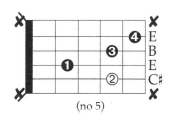

C#m7

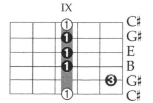
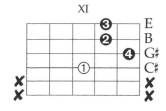

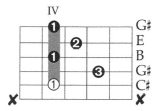
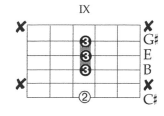

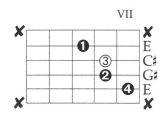

C#m6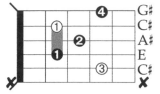

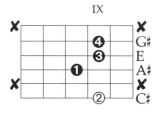

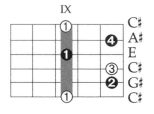

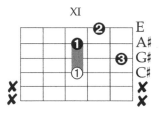

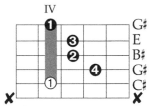

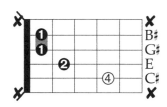

C#m(maj7)

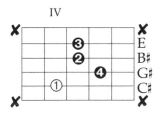

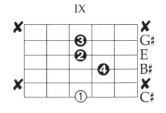

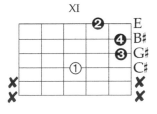

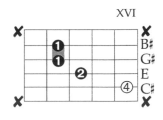

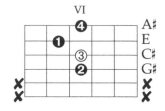

C#m add9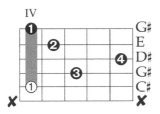

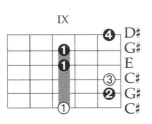

IX

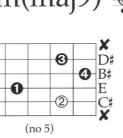

C#m9

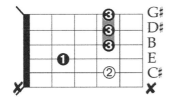

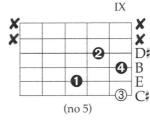
(no 5)

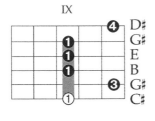

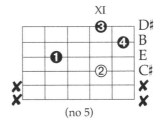
(no 5)

C#m(maj9)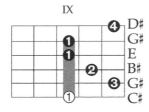

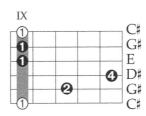
(no 5)

(no 5)

IX

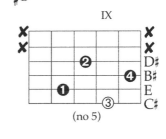

C#m$_9^6$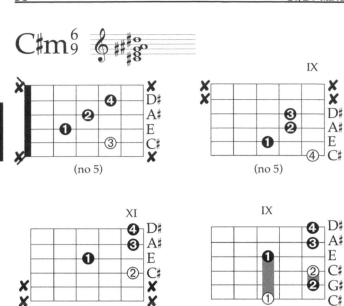

C#
D♭

(no 5)   (no 5)

(no 5)   (no 5)

C#m11(no9)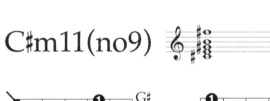

(no 5)

(no 5)

C#m11

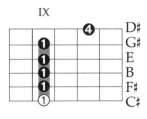
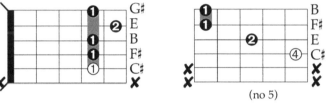
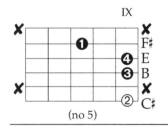

C#7

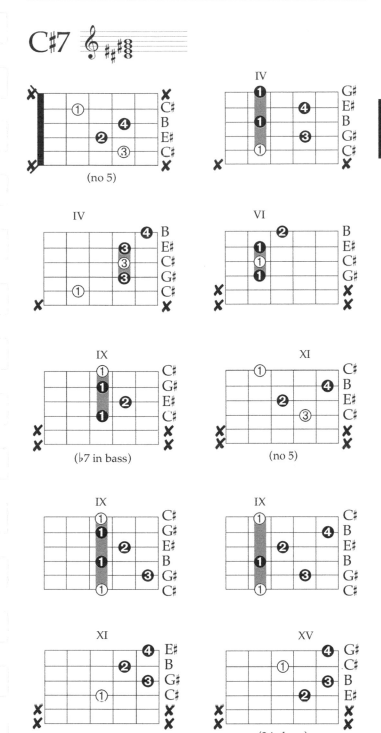

C#9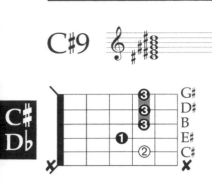

C#
D♭

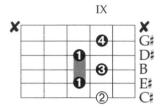

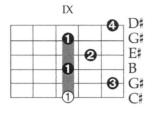

(no 5)

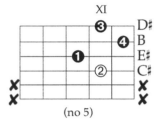

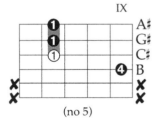

(no 5)

C#13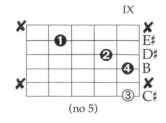

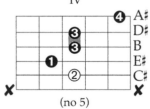

(no 5)

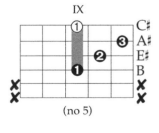

(no 5)

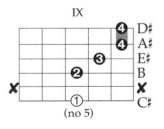

(no 5)

(no 5)

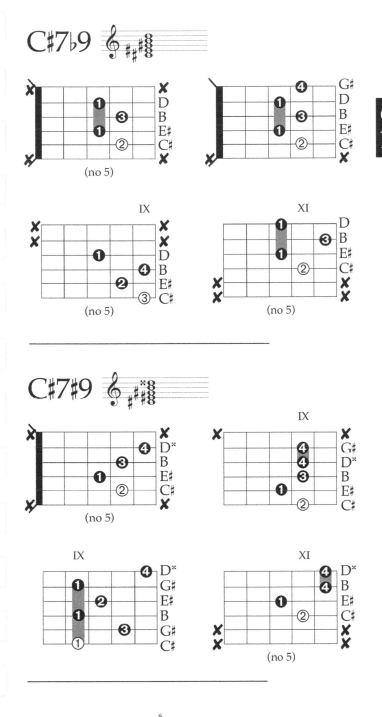

C#7♭9

(no 5)

IX

XI   (no 5)

C# / Db

C#7#9

IX

IX

XI   (no 5)

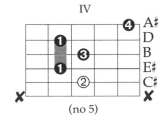

C#13♭9

IV   (no 5)

IX   (no 5)

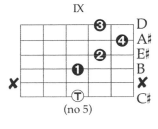

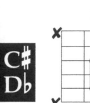 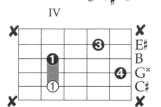

C♯7+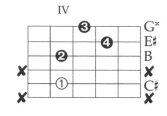

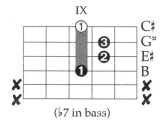 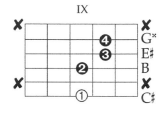

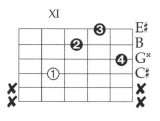

(♭7 in bass)

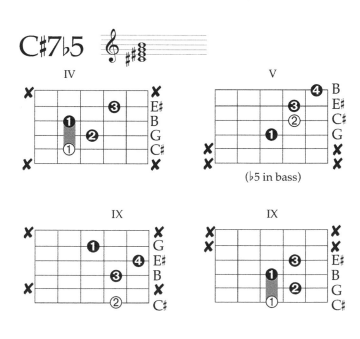

C♯7♭5

(♭5 in bass)

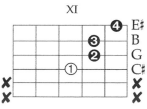

C#7♭9#5

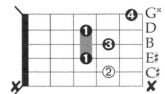

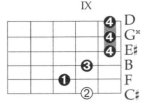

G×
D
B
E#
C#

IX

D
G×
E#
B
F
C#

___

C#7#9#5

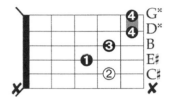

G×
D×
B
E#
C#

IX

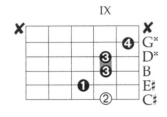

G×
D×
B
E#
C#

___

C#9#11

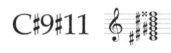

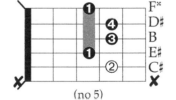

F×
D#
B
E#
C#

(no 5)

IX

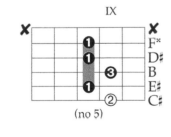

F×
D#
B
E#
C#

(no 5)

___

C#9+

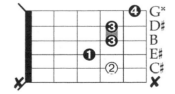

G×
D#
B
E#
C#

IX

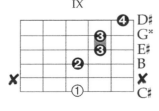

D#
G×
E#
B
C#

C#7sus4

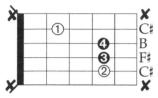
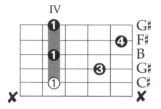

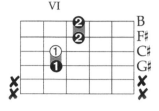
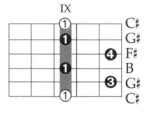

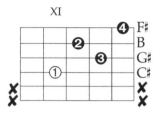
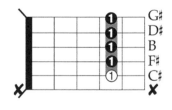

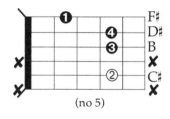

C#9sus4

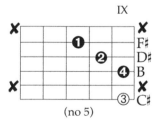
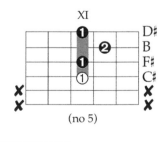

C#13sus4

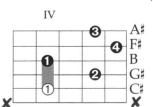
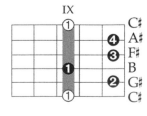

C#°

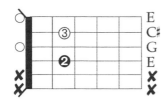

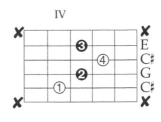

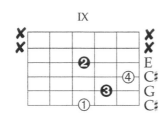

C#m7b5

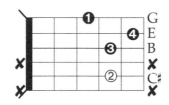

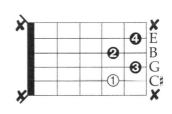

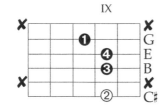

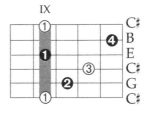

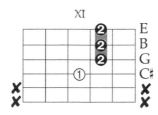

C#°7

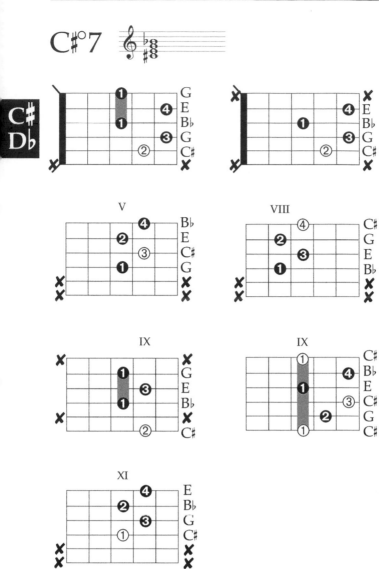

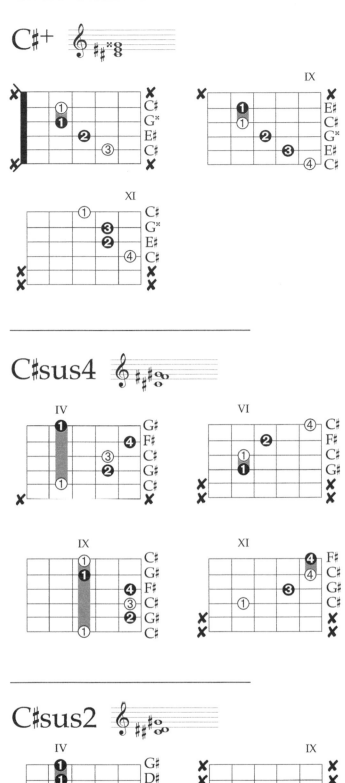

C#+

C#/Db

C#sus4

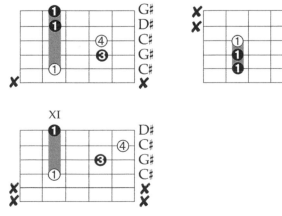

C#sus2

D

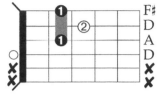
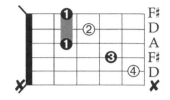

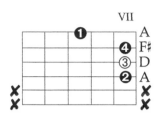
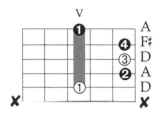

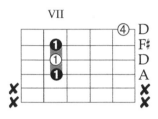
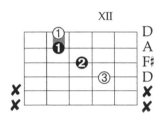

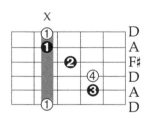
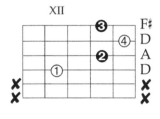

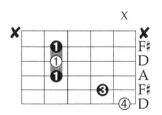
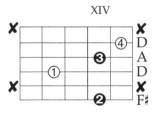

D6

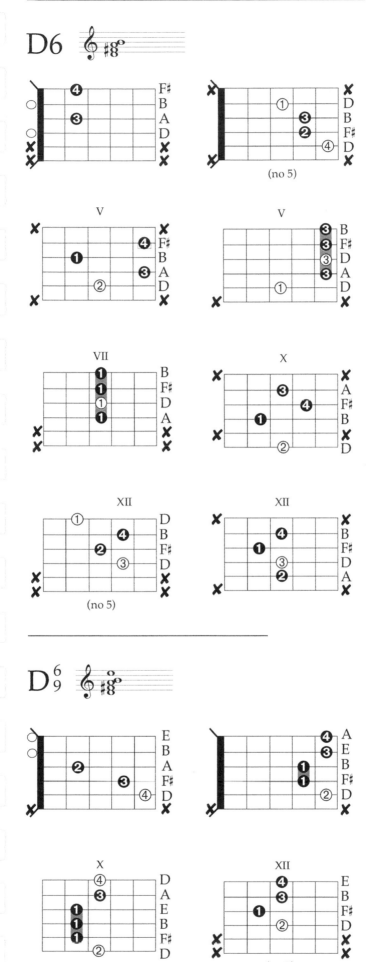

D6/9

D

Dmaj7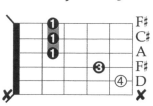

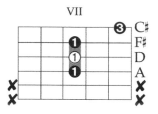

F#
C#
A
F#
D

V

A
F#
C#
A
D

VII

C#
F#
D
A

XII

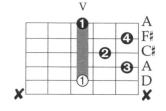

C#
A
F#
D

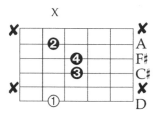 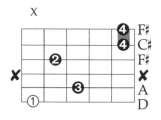

X

A
F#
C#
D

X

F#
C#
F#
A
D

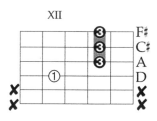

XII

F#
C#
A
D

Dmaj13

X

C#
A
E
B
F#
D

X

C#
B
E
C#
F#
D

(no 5)

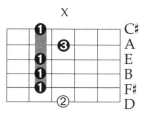 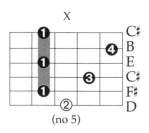

X

E
B
F#
C#
D

(no 5)

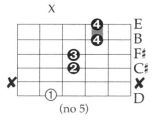

Dmaj9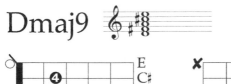

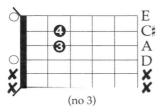

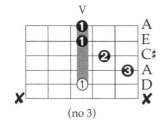

E
C#
A
D
X
X
(no 3)

V
X X
E
C#
F#
D
X
(no 5)

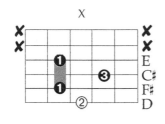

V
A
E
C#
A
D
X
(no 3)

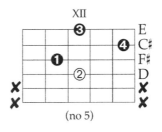

X
C#
A
E
C#
F#
D

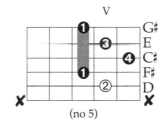

X X
X X
E
C#
F#
D

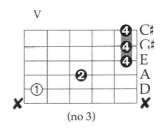

XII
E
C#
F#
D
X
X
(no 5)

D

Dmaj9#11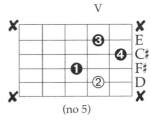

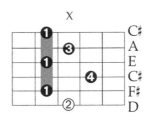

V
G#
E
C#
F#
D
X
(no 5)

V
C#
G#
E
A
D
X
(no 3)

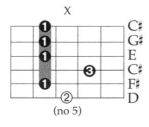

X
C#
G#
E
C#
F#
D
(no 5)

Dmaj7⁺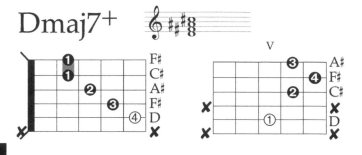

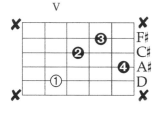

V

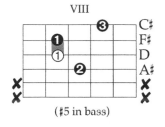

V

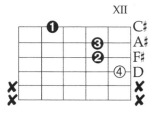

VIII

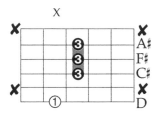

(♯5 in bass)

XII

X

Dmaj7♭5

V

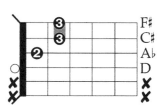

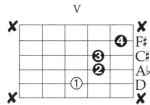

XII

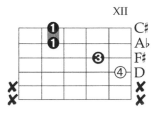

X

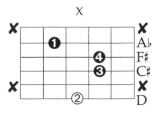

Dmaj13(no9)

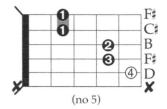

(no 5)

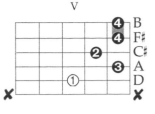

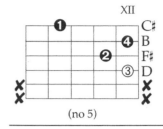

(no 5)

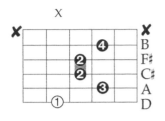

Dadd9

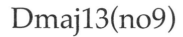

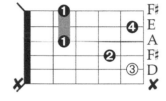

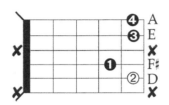

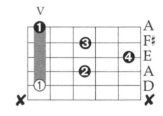

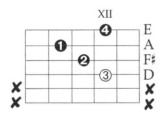

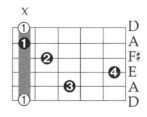

D

Dm

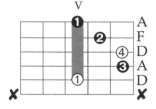

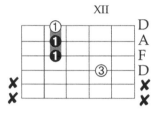

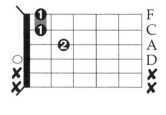

Dm7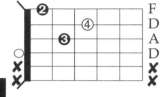

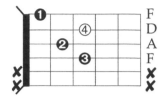

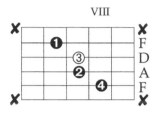

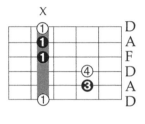

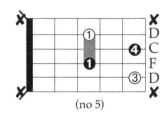

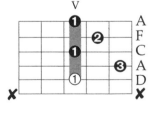

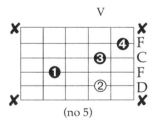

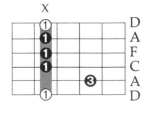

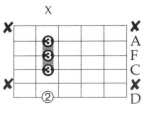

Dm6

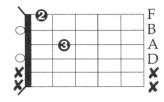

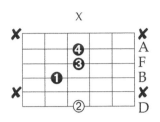

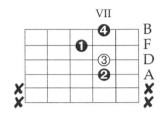

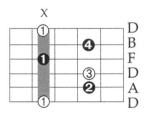

Dm(maj7)

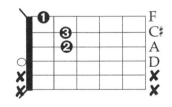

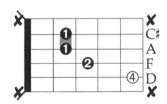

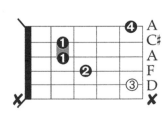

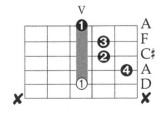

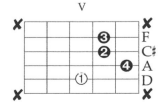

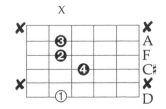

D

Dm add9

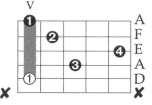

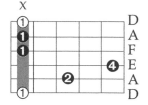

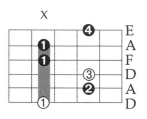

Dm9

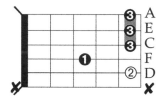

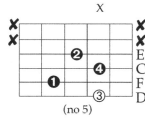

(no 5)

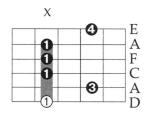

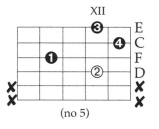

(no 5)

Dm(maj9)

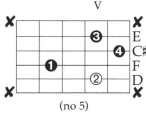

(no 5)

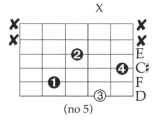

(no 5)

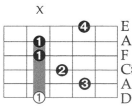

D

Dm$_9^6$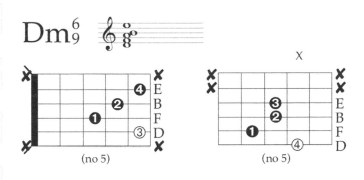

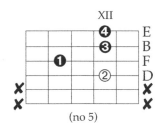
(no 5)

X

(no 5)

XII

(no 5)

X

D

Dm11(no9)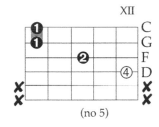

V

(no 5)

XII

(no 5)

X

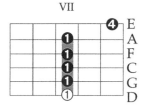
(no 5)

Dm11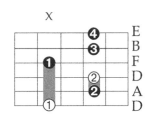

VII

D7

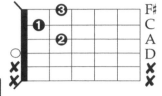

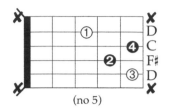

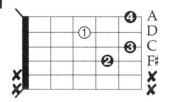

(no 5)

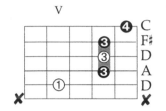

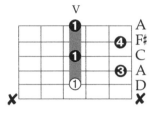

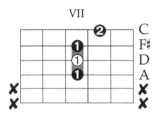

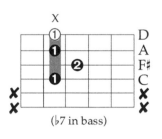

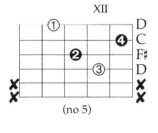

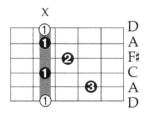

(♭7 in bass)

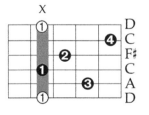

(no 5)

D9

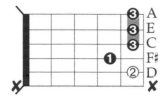

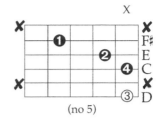

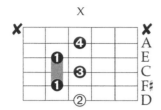

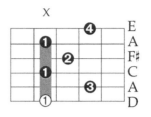

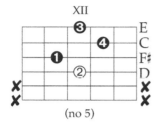

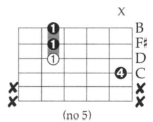

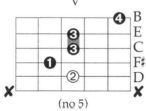

D

D13

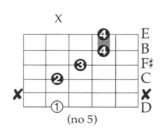

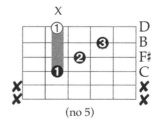

D7♭9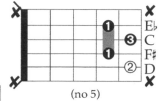

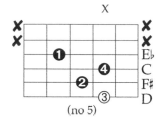

(no 5)

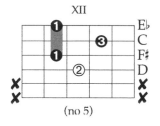

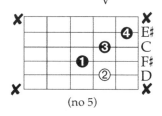

X

(no 5)

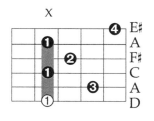

XII

(no 5)

D7♯9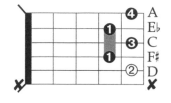

V

(no 5)

X

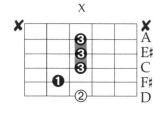

X

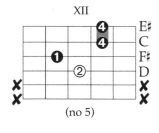

XII

(no 5)

D13♭9

V

(no 5)

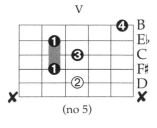

X

(no 5)

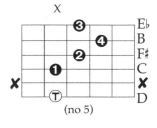

D7+

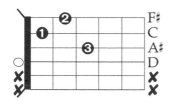

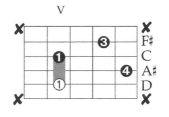

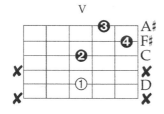

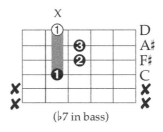

(♭7 in bass)

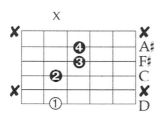

D7♭5

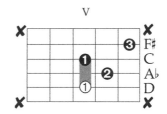

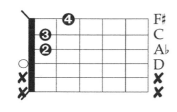

(♭5 in bass)

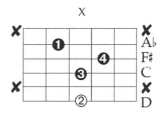

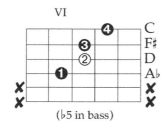

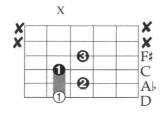

D

D7$^{\flat9}_{\sharp5}$
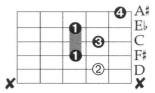
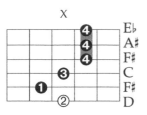

D7$^{\sharp9}_{\sharp5}$

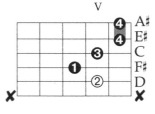
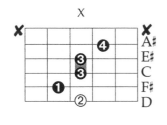

D9$\sharp$11

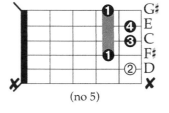
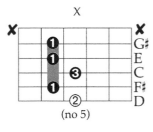

(no 5)   (no 5)

D9$^+$

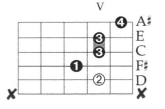
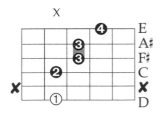

D7sus4

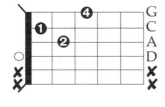

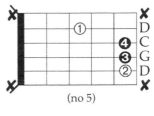
(no 5)

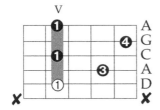

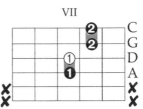

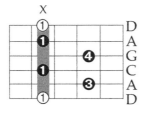

D9sus4

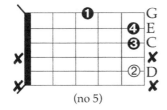
(no 5)

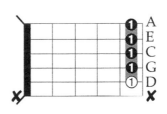

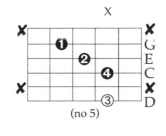
(no 5)

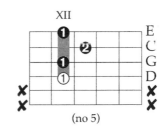
(no 5)

D13sus4

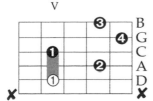

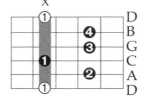

D

D°

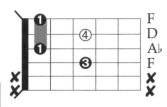

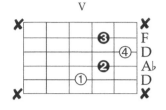

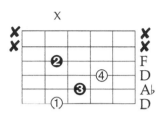

Dm7♭5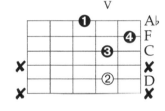

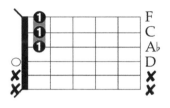

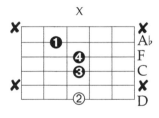

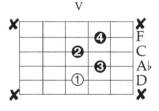

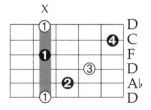

D°7

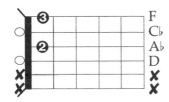

F
Cb
Ab
D
✗
✗

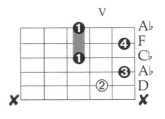

V

Ab
F
Cb
Ab
D
✗

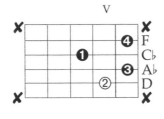

V

✗
F
Cb
Ab
D
✗

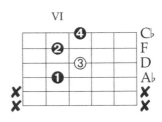

VI

Cb
F
D
Ab
✗
✗

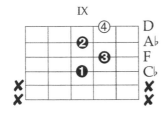

IX

D
Ab
F
Cb
✗
✗

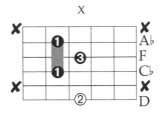

X

Ab
F
Cb
✗
D

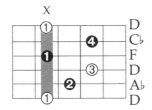

X

D
Cb
F
D
Ab
D

D

D+

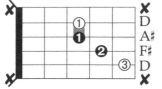

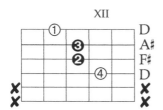

Dsus4

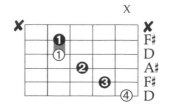

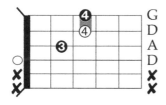

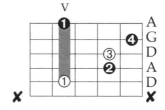

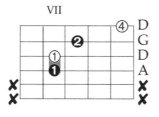

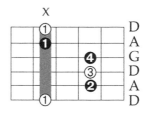

Dsus2

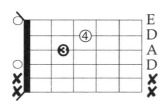

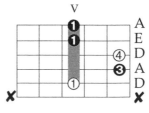

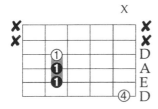

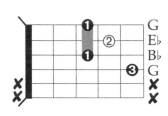

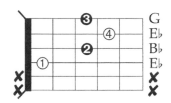

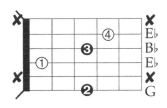

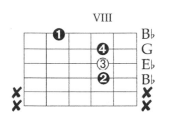

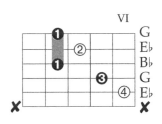

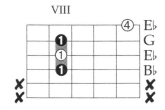

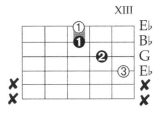

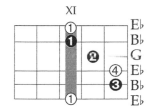

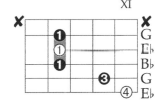

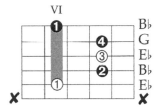

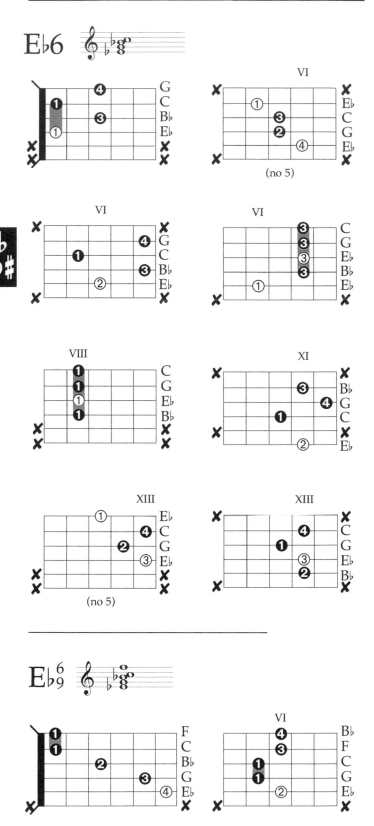

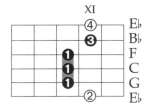

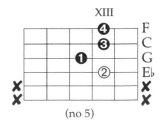

E♭maj7

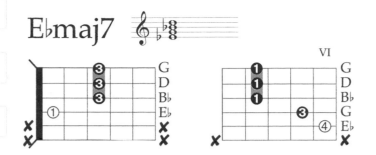

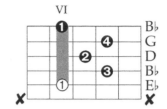

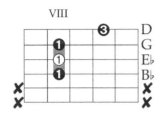

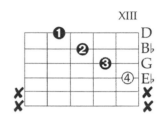

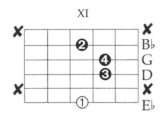

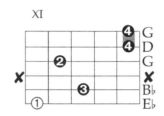

E♭maj13

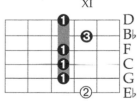

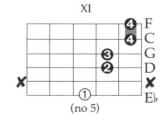

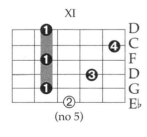

E♭maj9

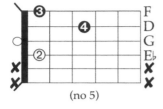

(no 5)

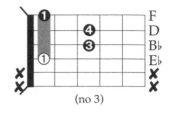

(no 3)

VI

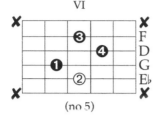

(no 5)

VI

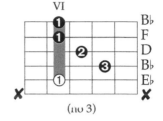

(no 3)

XI

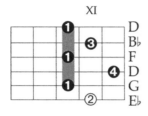

XI

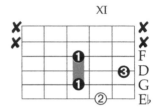

E♭maj9♯11

VI

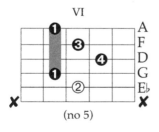

(no 5)

VI

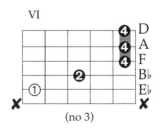

(no 3)

XI

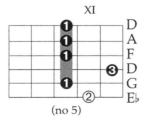

(no 5)

E♭maj7+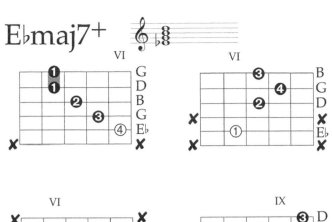

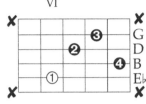

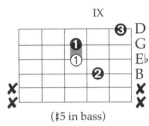

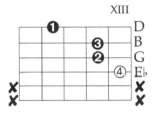

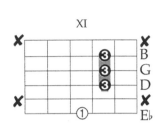

(♯5 in bass)

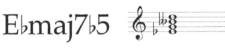

Eb
D#

E♭maj7♭5

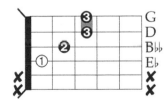

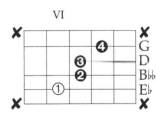

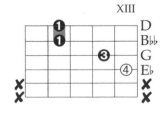

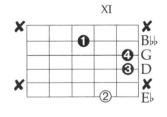

E♭maj13(no9)

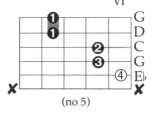

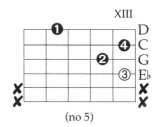

E♭add9

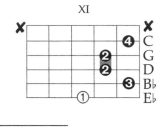

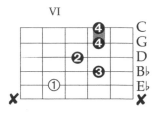

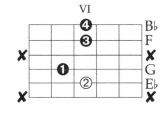

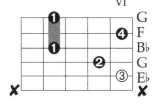

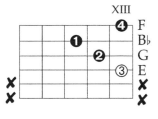

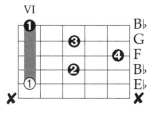

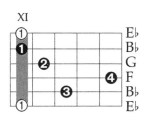

The Gig Bag Book of GuitarTab Chords   69

E♭m

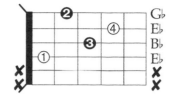

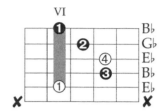

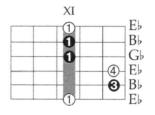

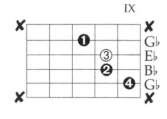

E♭ / D♯

E♭m7

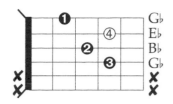

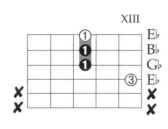

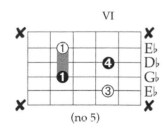

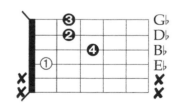

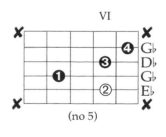

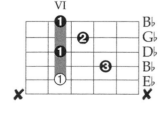

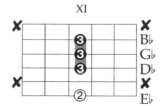

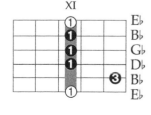

Ebm6

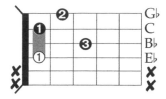

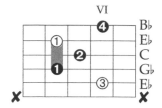

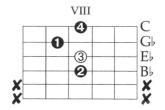

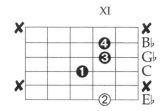

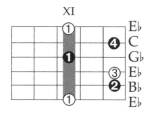

Ebm(maj7)

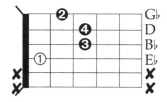

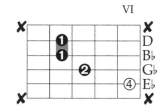

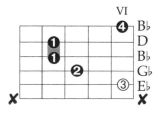

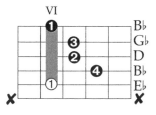

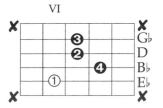

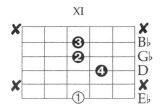

E♭m add9

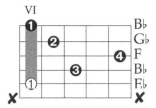

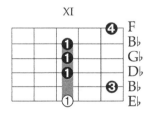

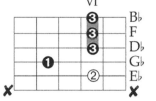

E♭m9

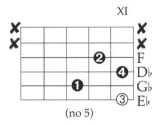

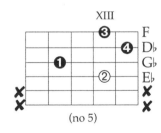

E♭m(maj9)

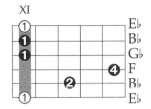

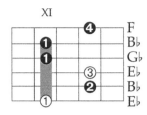

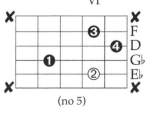

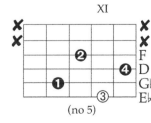

E♭m⁶₉

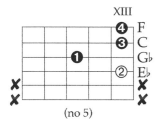

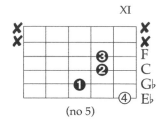

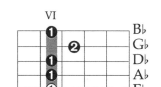

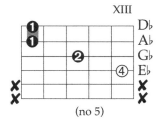

E♭m11(no9)

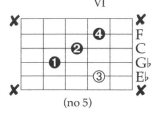

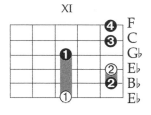

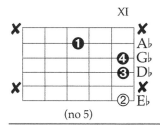

E♭m11

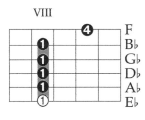

E♭7

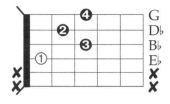
G
D♭
B♭
E♭

VI

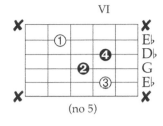
E♭
D♭
G
E♭

(no 5)

E♭
D#

V

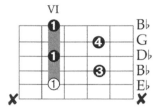
B♭
E♭
D♭
G

(3 in bass)

VI

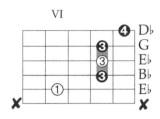
D♭
G
E♭
B♭
E♭

VI

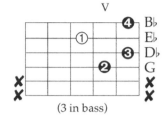
B♭
G
D♭
B♭
E♭

VIII

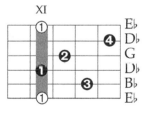
D♭
G
E♭
B♭

XI

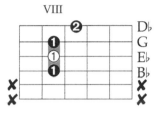
E♭
B♭
G
D♭

(♭7 in bass)

XIII

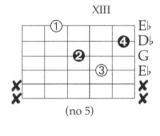
E♭
D♭
G
E♭

(no 5)

XI

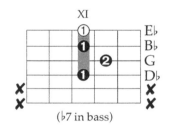
E♭
B♭
G
D♭
B♭
E♭

XI

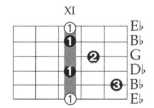
E♭
D♭
G
D♭
B♭
E♭

E♭9

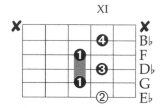

VI
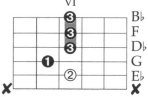
B♭
F
D♭
G
E♭

XI
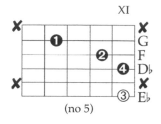
G
F
D♭
E♭
(no 5)

XI
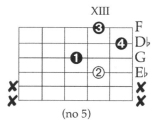
B♭
F
D♭
G
E♭

XI
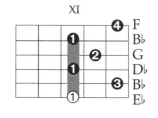
F
B♭
G
D♭
B♭
E♭

XIII
F
D♭
G
E♭
(no 5)

E♭13

VI
(no 5)
C
F
D♭
G
E♭

XI
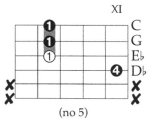
C
G
E♭
D♭
(no 5)

XI
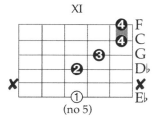
F
C
G
D♭
E♭
(no 5)

XI
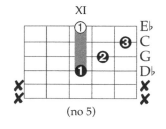
E♭
C
G
D♭
(no 5)

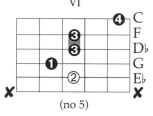

Eb7b9
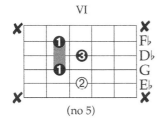
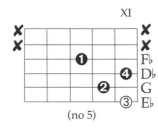

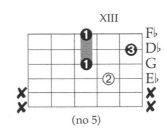

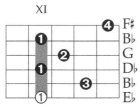

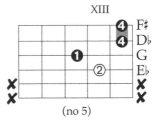

Eb7#9
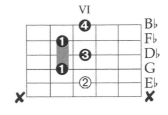

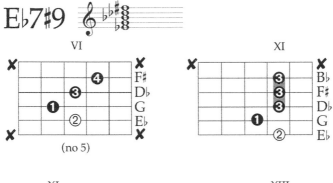

Eb13b9

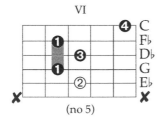

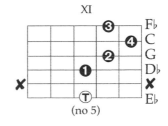

Eb7+

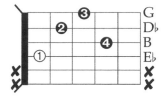

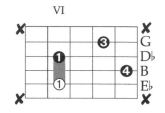

VI

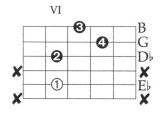

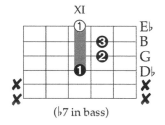
(b7 in bass)

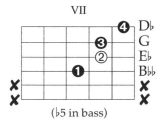

Eb7b5

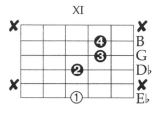

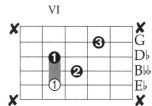

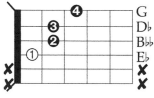
(b5 in bass)

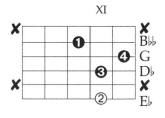

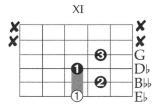

E♭7♭9#5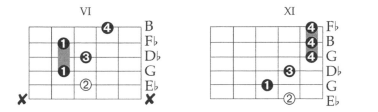

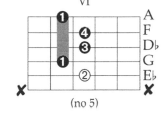

E♭7#9#5

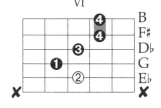

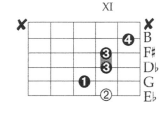

E♭9#11

(no 5)   (no 5)

E♭9+

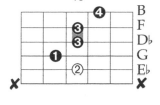

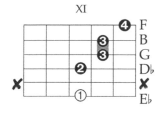

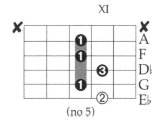

Eb7sus4

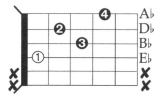

Ab
Db
Bb
Eb
✗
✗

VI

✗
Eb
Db
Ab
Eb

(no 5)

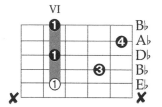

VI

Bb
Ab
Db
Bb
Eb

VIII

Db
Ab
Eb
Bb

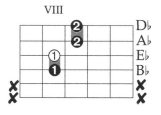

XI

Eb
Bb
Ab
Db
Bb
Eb

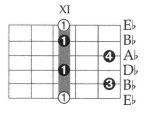

Eb9sus4

F
Db
Ab
Eb
✗
✗

VI

Ab
F
Db
✗
Eb
✗

(no 5)   (no 5)

VI

Bb
F
Db
Ab
Eb
✗

XI

✗
Ab
F
Db
✗
Eb

(no 5)

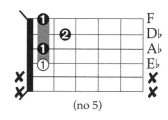 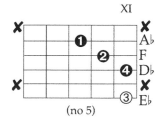

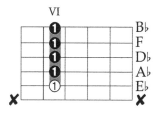

Eb13sus4

VI

C
Ab
Db
Bb
Eb

XI

Eb
C
Ab
Db
Bb
Eb

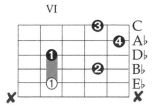 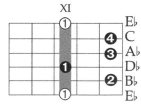

E♭°

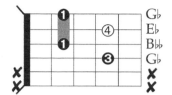
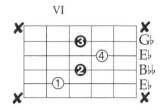

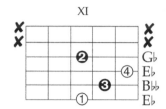

E♭m7♭5

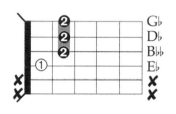

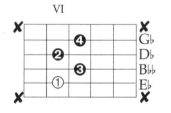
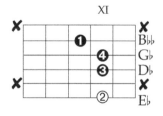

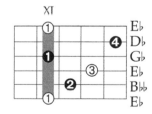

E♭°7

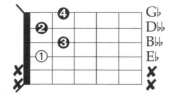

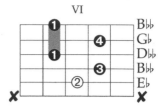

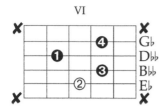

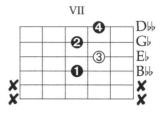

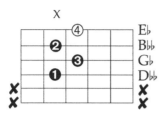

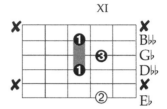

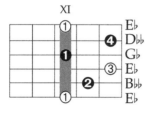

Eb+

VI

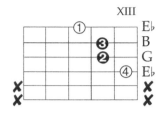

XI

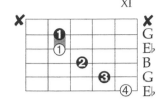

XIII

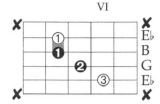

Eb
D#

Ebsus4

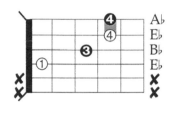

VI

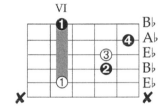

VIII

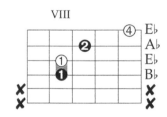

XI

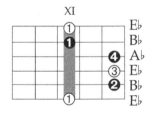

Ebsus2

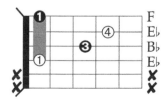

VI

XI

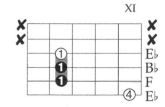

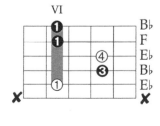

E

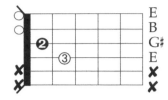

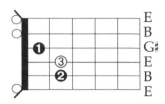

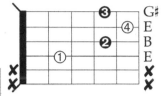

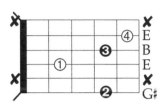

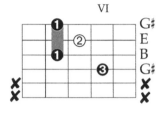

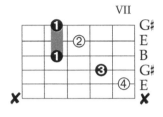

E

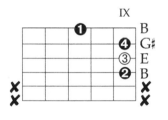

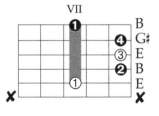

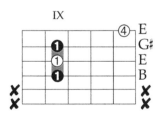

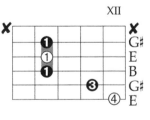

E6

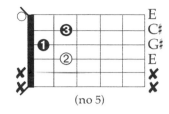

E
C#
G#
E
X
X

(no 5)

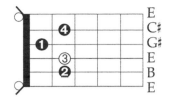

E
C#
G#
E
B
E

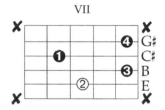

G#
C#
B
E
X
X

VII

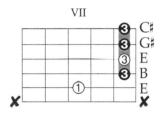

X
E
C#
G#
E
X

(no 5)

VII

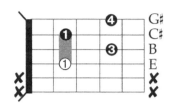

X
G#
C#
B
E
X

VII

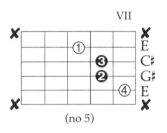

C#
G#
E
B
E
X

IX

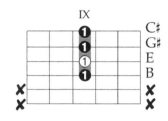

C#
G#
E
B
X
X

XII

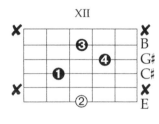

X
B
G#
C#
X
E

E

E $_9^6$

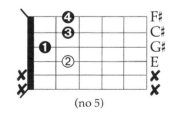

F#
C#
G#
E
X
X

(no 5)

II

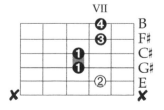

F#
C#
B
G#
E
X

VII

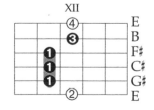

B
F#
C#
G#
E
X

XII

E
B
F#
C#
G#
E

Emaj7

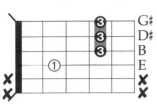

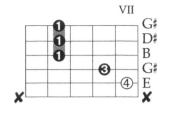

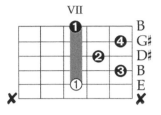

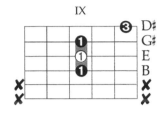

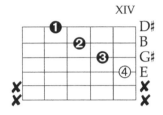

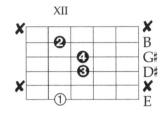

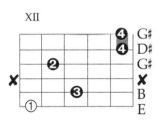

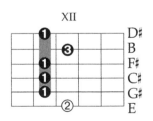

Emaj13

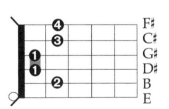

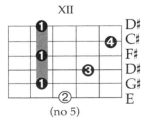

E

Emaj9

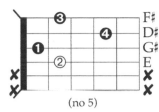

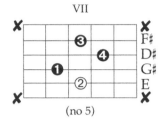

(no 5)

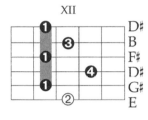

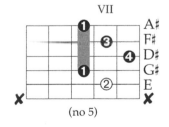

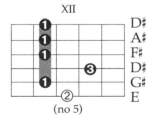

E

Emaj9#11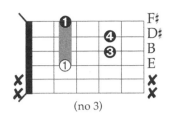

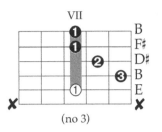

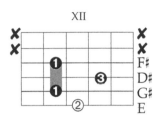

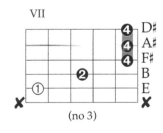

Emaj7+

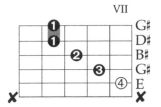 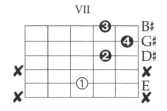

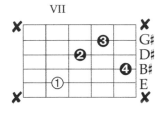 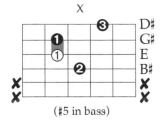

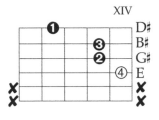 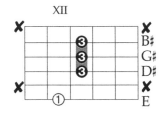

(#5 in bass)

Emaj7♭5

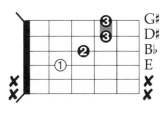 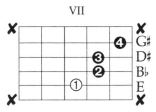

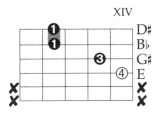 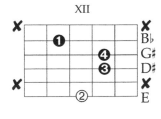

Emaj13(no9)

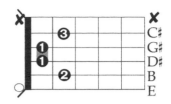

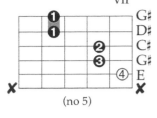

(no 5)

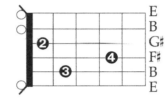

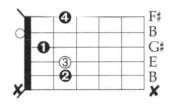

(no 5)

Eadd9

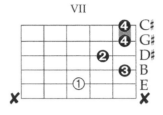

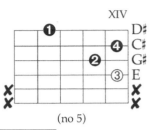

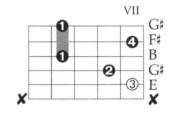

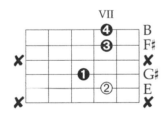

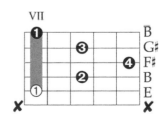

Em

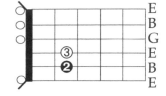
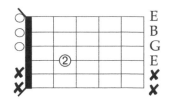

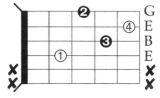
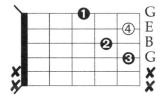

E

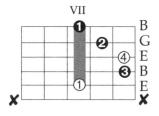
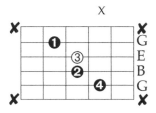

VII   X

Em7

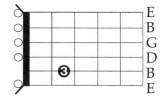
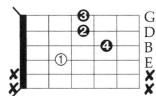

VII   VII

(no 5)   (no 5)

VII   XII

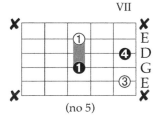
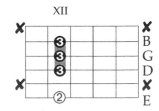

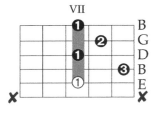
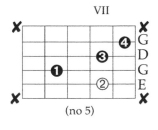

Em6

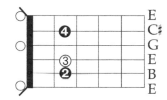
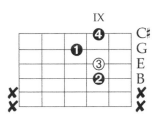

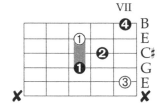

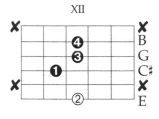

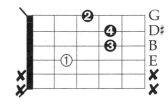

Em(maj7)

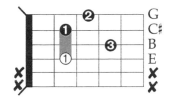

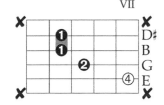

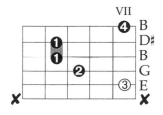

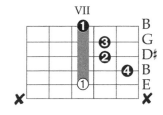

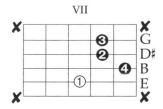

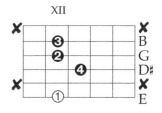

E

Em add9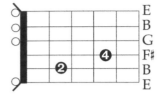

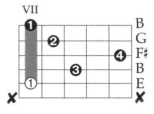

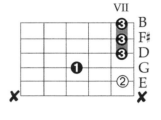

Em9

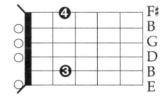

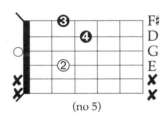

Em(maj9)

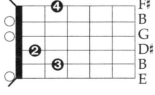

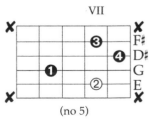

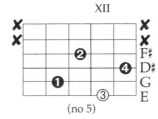

Em$^6_9$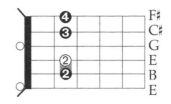

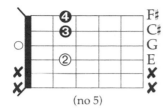
(no 5)

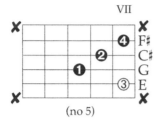

Em11(no9)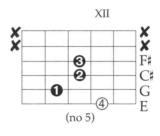

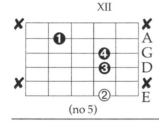
(no 5)

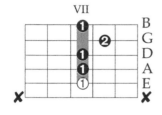

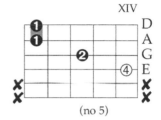
(no 5)

Em11

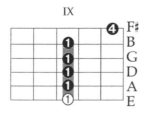

E

E7

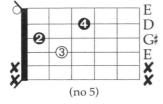
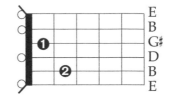

(no 5)

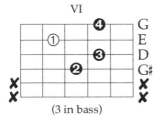
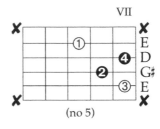

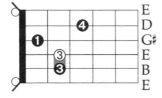
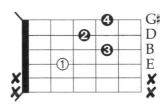

(no 5)

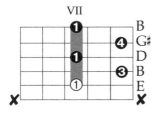
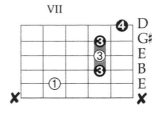

(3 in bass)

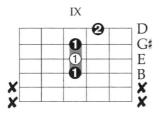
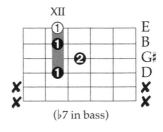

(♭7 in bass)

E

E9

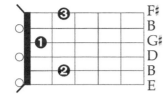

F#
B
G#
D
B
E

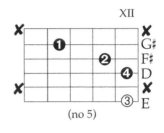

F#
D
G#
E
X
X

(no 5)

VII

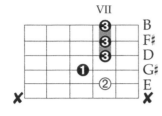

B
F#
D
G#
E
X

XII

F#
G#
F#
D
X
E

(no 5)

XII

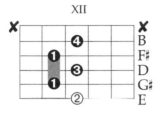

X
B
F#
D
G#
E

E13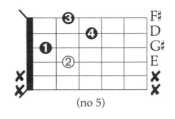

F#
C#
G#
D
B
E

VII

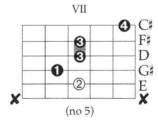

C#
F#
D
G#
E
X

(no 5)

XII

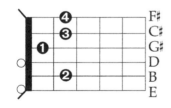

C#
G#
E
D
X
X

(no 5)

XII

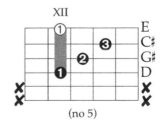

E
C#
G#
D
X
X

(no 5)

E

E7♭9
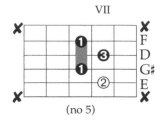

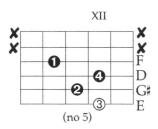

(no 5)

VII

(no 5)

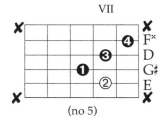

VII

XII

(no 5)

E

E7♯9
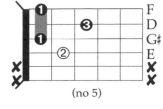

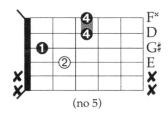

(no 5)

VII

(no 5)

XII

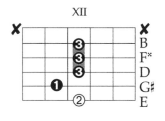

E13♭9
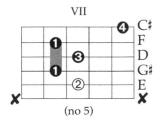

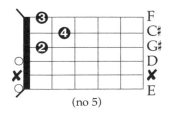

(no 5)

VII

(no 5)

E7+

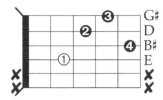

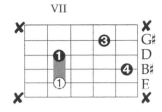

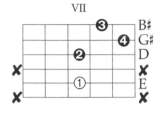

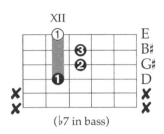

(♭7 in bass)

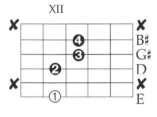

E7♭5

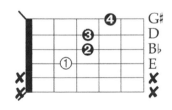

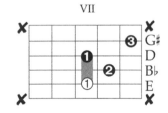

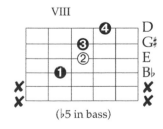

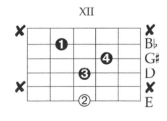

(♭5 in bass)

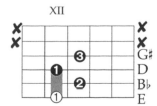

E

E7♭9#5

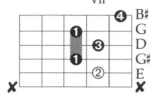

E7#9#5

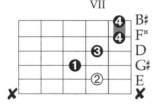

E9#11

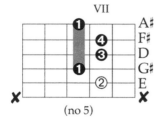
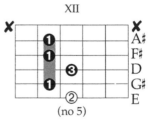

(no 5)   (no 5)

E9+

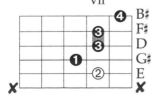
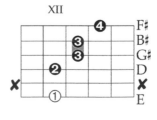

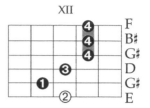

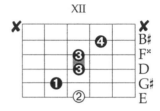

E7sus4

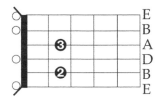
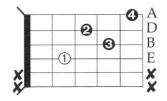

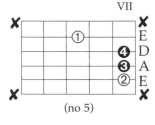
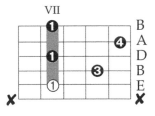

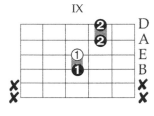

E9sus4

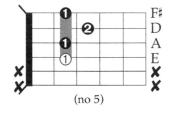
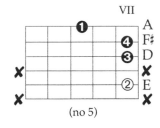

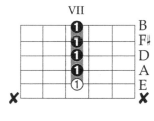
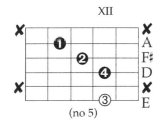

E

E13sus4

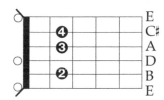
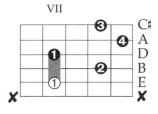

E°

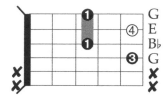

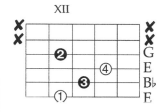

E

Em7♭5

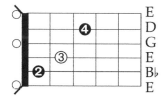
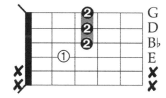

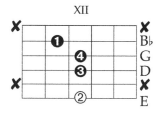
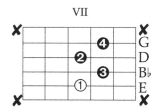

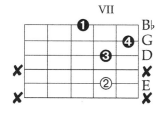
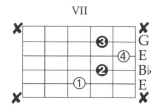

E°7

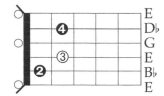

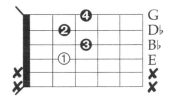

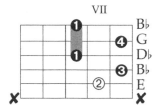

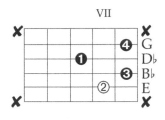

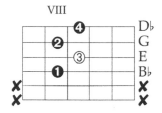

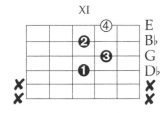

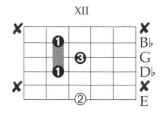

E

E+

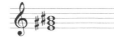

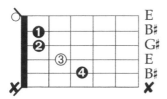

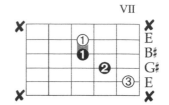

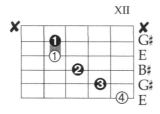

E

Esus4

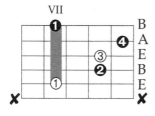

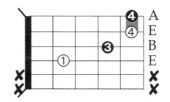

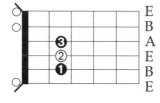

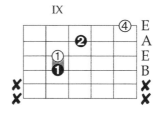

Esus2

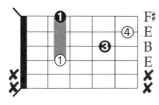

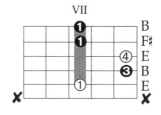

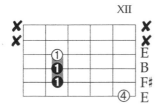

F

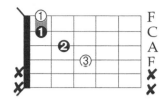

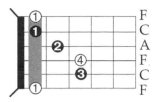

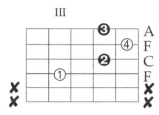

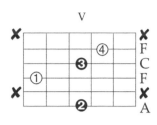

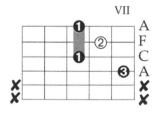

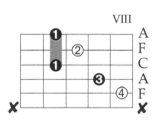

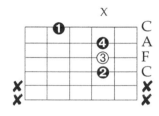

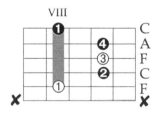

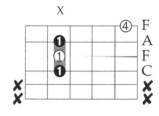

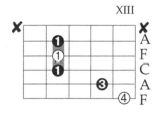

F

F6

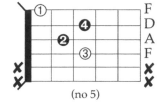

F
D
A
F

(no 5)

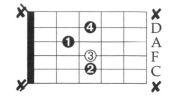

D
A
F
C

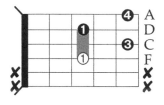

A
D
C
F

VIII

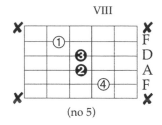

F
D
A
F

(no 5)

VIII

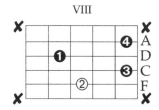

A
D
C
F

VIII

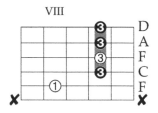

D
A
F
C
F

X

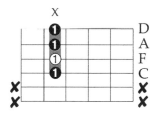

D
A
F
C

XI

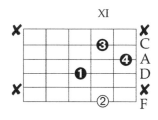

C
A
D
F

F $\frac{6}{9}$

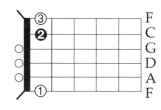

F
C
G
D
A
F

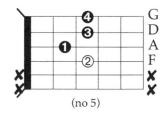

G
D
A
F

(no 5)

VIII

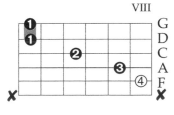

G
D
C
A
F

VIII

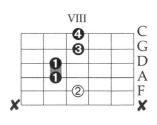

C
G
D
A
F

Fmaj7

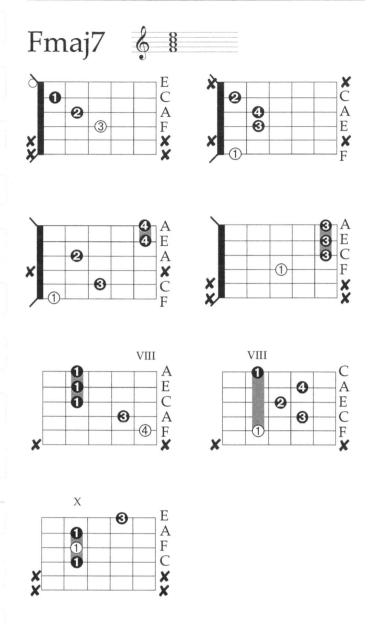

Fmaj13

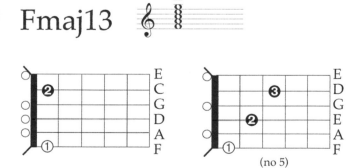

(no 5)

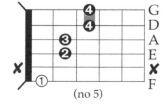

(no 5)

Fmaj9

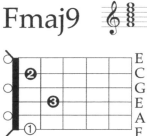

E
C
G
E
A
F

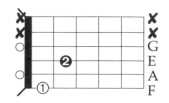

G
E
A
F

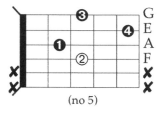

G
E
A
F
(no 5)

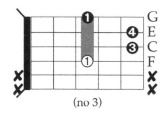

G
E
C
F
(no 3)

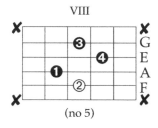

VIII

G
E
A
F
(no 5)

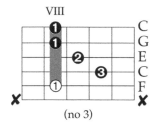

VIII

C
G
E
C
F
(no 3)

Fmaj9♯11

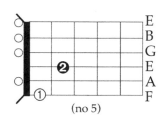

E
B
G
E
A
F
(no 5)

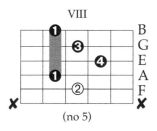

VIII

B
G
E
A
F
(no 5)

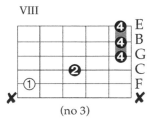

VIII

E
B
G
C
F
(no 3)

Fmaj7+

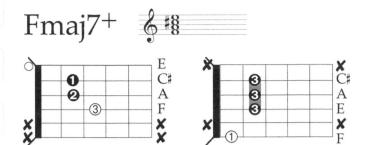

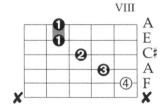

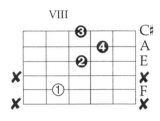

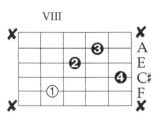

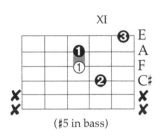

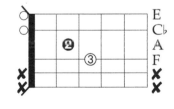

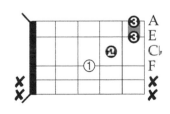

(♯5 in bass)

Fmaj7♭5

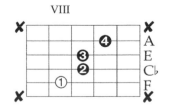

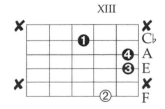

F

Fmaj13(no9)

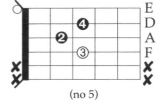

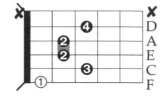

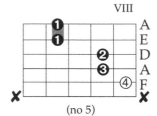

(no 5)

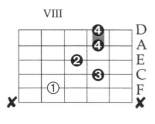

VIII

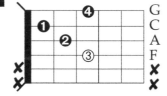

(no 5)

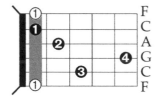

VIII

Fadd9

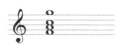

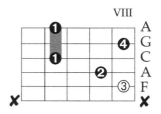

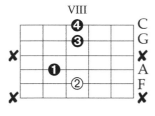

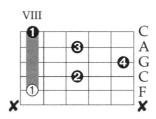

VIII

VIII

VIII

Fm

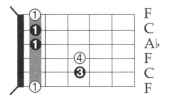
F
C
A♭
F
C
F

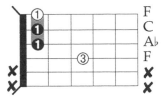
F
C
A♭
F

III
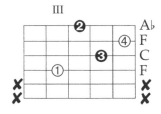
A♭
F
C
F

VI
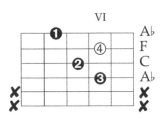
A♭
F
C
A♭

VIII
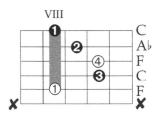
C
A♭
F
C
F

XI
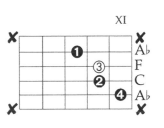
A♭
F
C
A♭

F

Fm7

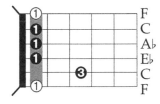
F
C
A♭
E♭
C
F

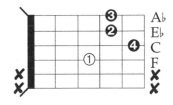
A♭
E♭
C
F

VIII
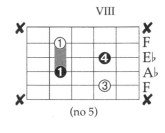
F
E♭
A♭
F
(no 5)

VIII
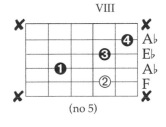
A♭
E♭
A♭
F
(no 5)

VIII
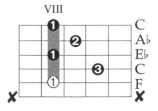
C
A♭
E♭
C
F

XIII
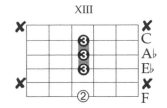
C
A♭
E♭
F

Fm6

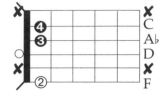

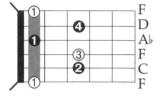

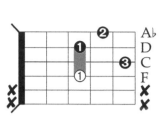

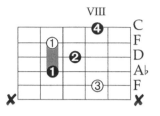

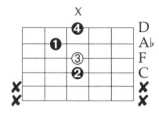

Fm(maj7)

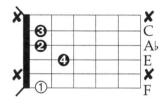

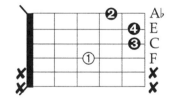

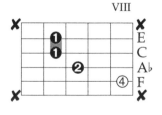

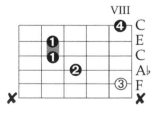

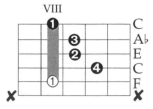

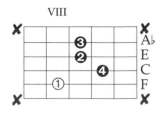

F

Fm add9

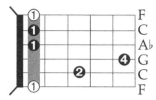
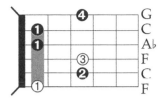

Fm9

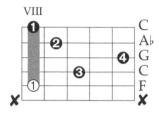
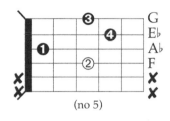

(no 5)

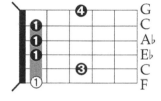
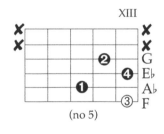

(no 5)

(no 5)

Fm(maj9)

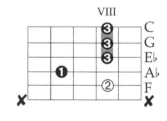
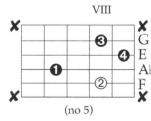

(no 5)

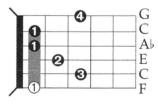

(no 5)

F

Fm⁶₉

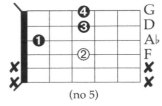

(no 5)

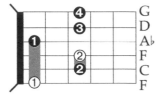

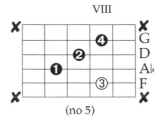

VIII

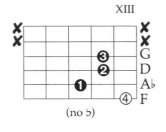

(no 5)   (no ♭)

Fm11(no9)

VIII

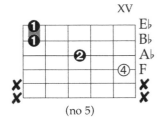

XV

(no 5)

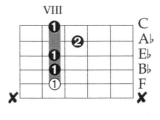

XIII

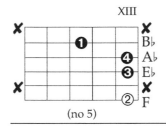

(no 5)

Fm11

X

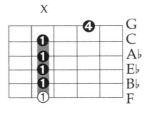

F7

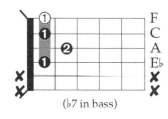
(♭7 in bass)

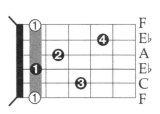
(no 5)

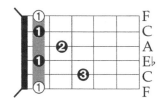

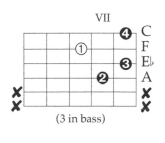

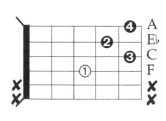

VII

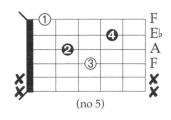
(3 in bass)

VIII

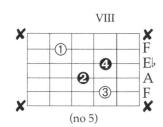
(no 5)

VIII

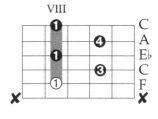

VIII

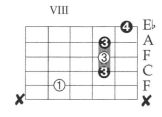

X

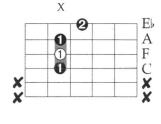

F

F9

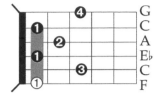

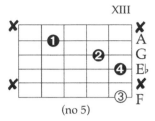

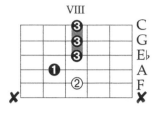

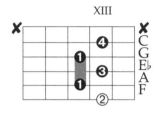

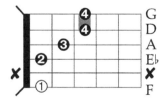

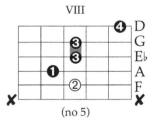

F13

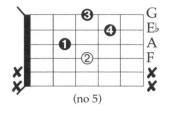

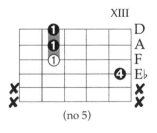

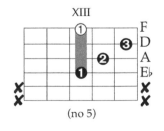

F7♭9

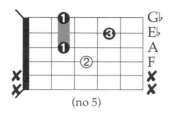 (no 5)

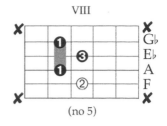
VIII
(no 5)

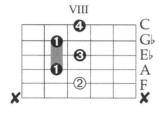
VIII
(no 5)

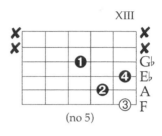
XIII
(no 5)

F7♯9

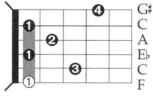

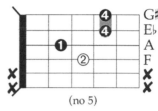 (no 5)

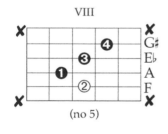
VIII
(no 5)

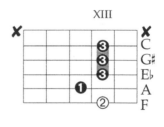
XIII

F13♭9

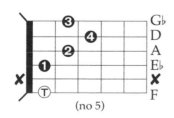 (no 5)

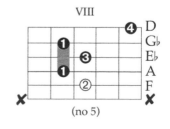
VIII
(no 5)

F

F7+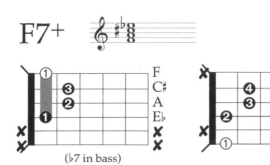

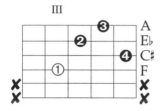

F
C#
A
Eb
✗
✗

(b7 in bass)

✗
C#
A
Eb
✗
F

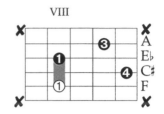

III

A
Eb
C#
F
✗
✗

VIII

✗
A
Eb
C#
F
✗

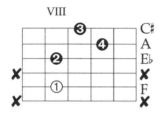
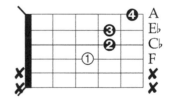

VIII

C#
A
Eb
✗
F
✗

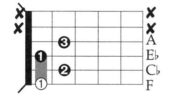

F7b5

✗
✗
A
Eb
Cb
F

A
Eb
Cb
F
✗
✗

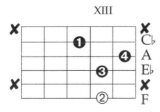

VIII

✗
A
Eb
Cb
F
✗

IX

Eb
A
F
Cb
✗
✗

(b5 in bass)

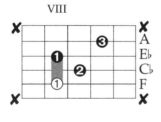
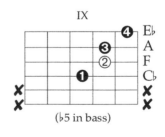

XIII

✗
Cb
A
Eb
✗
F

F7$^{\flat 9}_{\sharp 5}$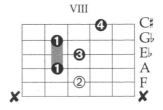

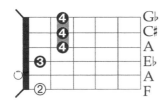

F7$^{\sharp 9}_{\sharp 5}$

F

F9$\sharp$11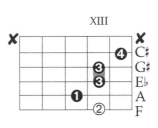

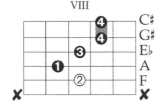

F9+

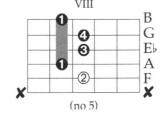 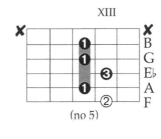

 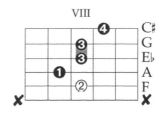

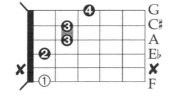

F7sus4

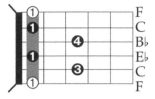

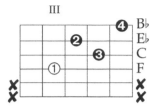

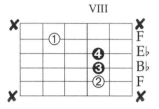

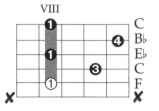

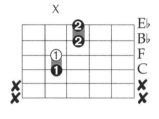

F

F9sus4

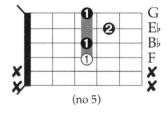

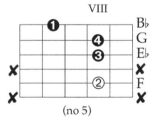

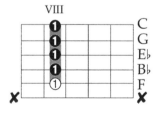

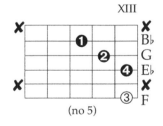

F13sus4

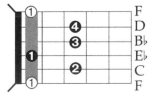

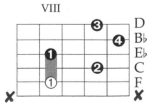

F°

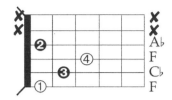

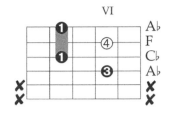

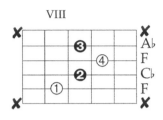

Fm7♭5

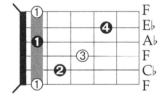

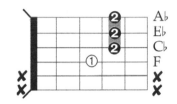

F

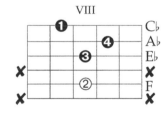

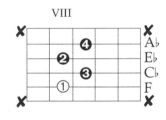

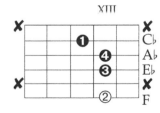

F°7

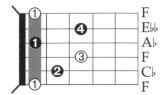

F
E♭♭
A♭
F
C♭
F

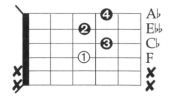

A♭
E♭♭
C♭
F
✗
✗

VIII

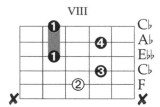

C♭
A♭
E♭♭
C♭
F

VIII

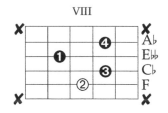

A♭
E♭♭
C♭
F

IX

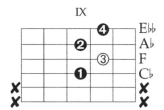

E♭♭
A♭
F
C♭

XII

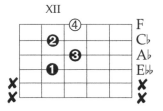

F
C♭
A♭
E♭♭

XIII

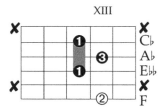

C♭
A♭
E♭♭
F

F

F+

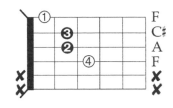

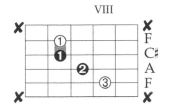

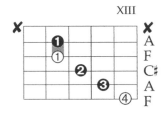

Fsus4

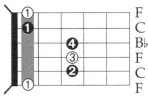

F

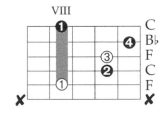

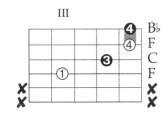

Fsus2

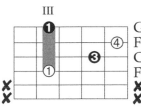

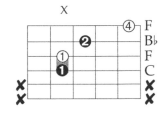

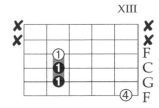

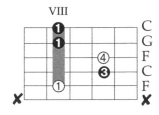

F#

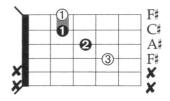

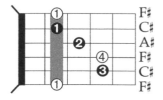

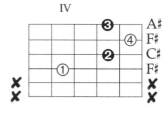

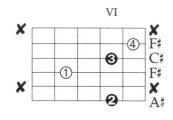

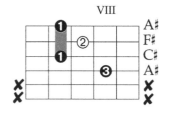

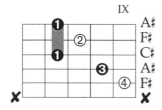

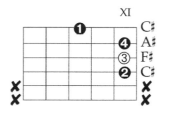

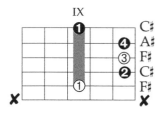

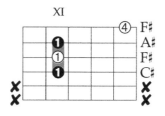

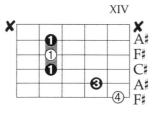

F#6

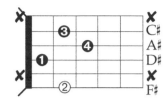

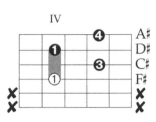

(no 5)

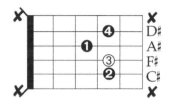

IV

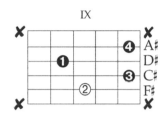

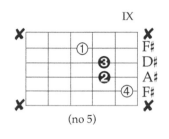

(no 5)

IX

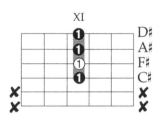

IX

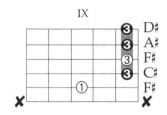

IX

XI

F#⁶₉

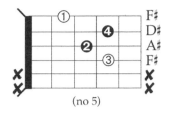

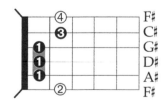

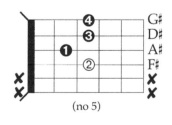

(no 5)

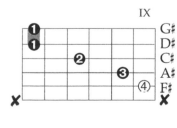

IX

IX

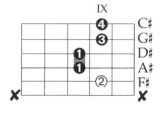

F#maj7

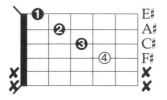

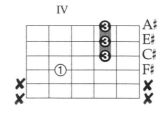

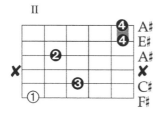

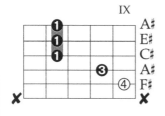

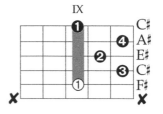

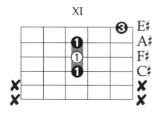

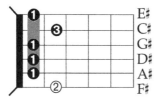

F#maj13

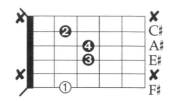

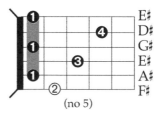

(no 5)

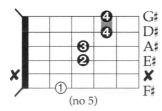

(no 5)

F#maj9

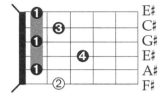

E#
C#
G#
E#
A#
F#

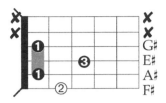

G#
E#
A#
F#

IV

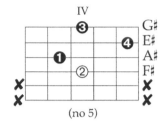

G#
E#
A#
F#

(no 5)

IV

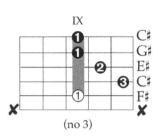

G#
E#
C#
F#

(no 3)

IX

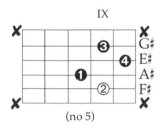

G#
E#
A#
F#

(no 5)

IX

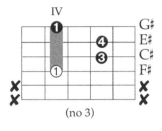

C#
G#
E#
C#
F#

(no 3)

F#maj9#11

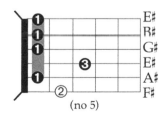

E#
B#
G#
E#
A#
F#

(no 5)

IX

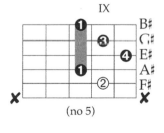

B#
C#
E#
A#
F#

(no 5)

IX

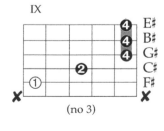

E#
B#
G#
C#
F#

(no 3)

F♯maj7+

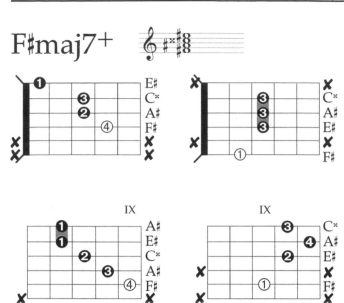

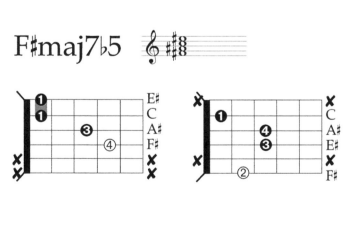

(♯5 in bass)

F♯maj7♭5

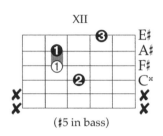

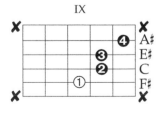

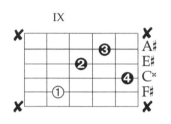

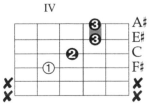

F♯
G♭

F#maj13(no9)

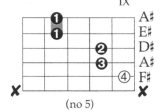

(no 5)

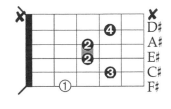

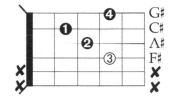

(no 5)

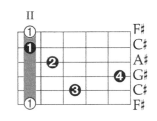

F#add9

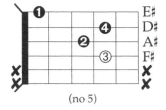

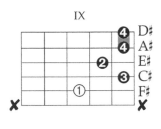

F#
Gb

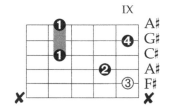

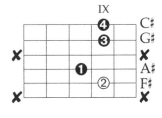

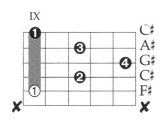

F#m

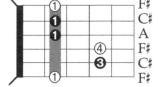
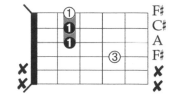

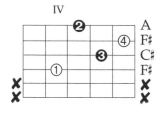
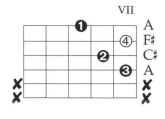

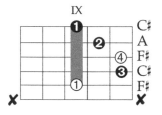
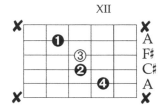

F#m7

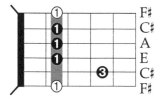
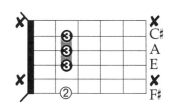

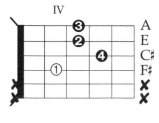
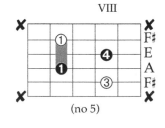

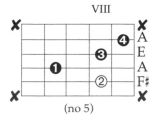
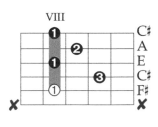

F#m6

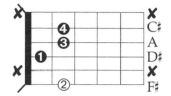

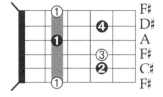

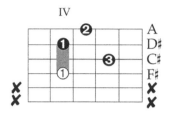

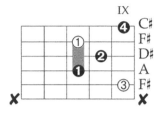

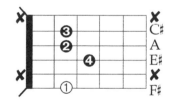

F#m(maj7)

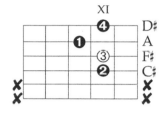

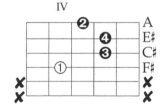

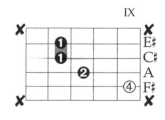

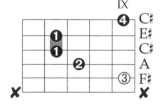

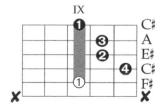

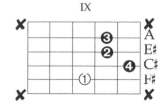

F#
Gb

F#m add9

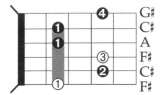

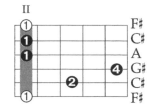

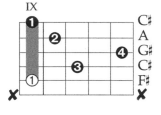

F#m9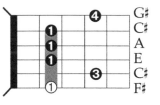

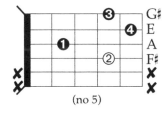

(no 5)

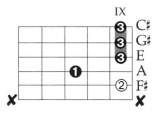

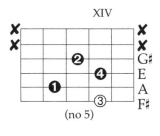

(no 5)

F#m(maj9)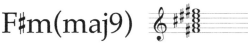

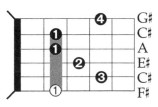

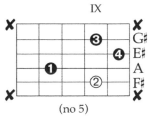

(no 5)

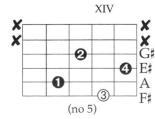

(no 5)

F#m⁶₉

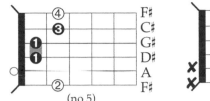
(no 5)

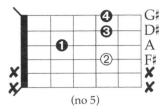
(no 5)

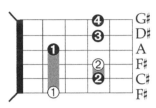

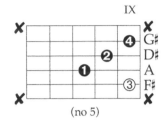
(no 5)

F#m11(no9)

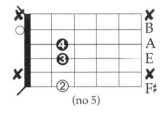
(no 5)

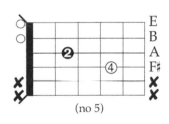
(no 5)

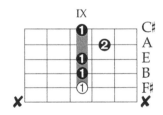

F#m11

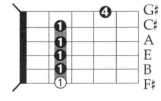

F#7

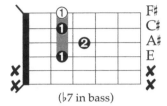

(♭7 in bass)

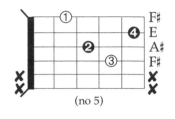

(no 5)

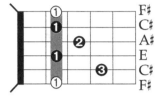

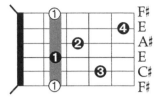

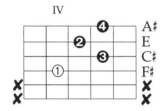

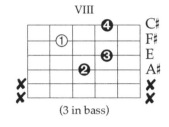

IV

VIII

(3 in bass)

F#
G♭

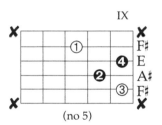

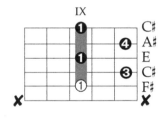

IX

(no 5)

IX

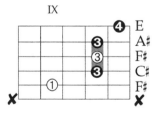

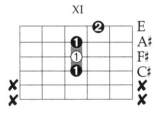

IX

XI

F#9

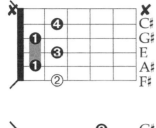
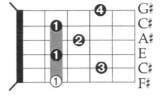

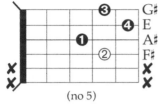
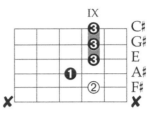

(no 5)

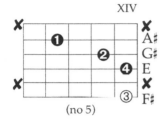

(no 5)

F#
Gb

F#13

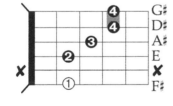
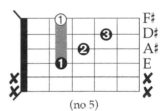

(no 5)

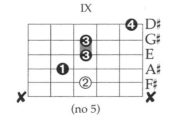
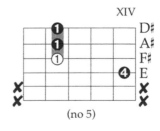

(no 5)   (no 5)

F#7♭9

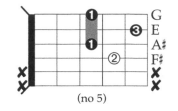

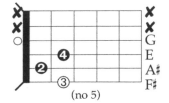
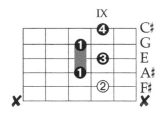

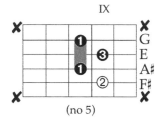

F#7#9

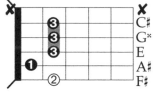
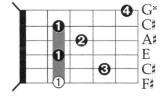

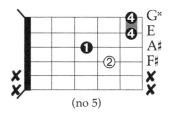
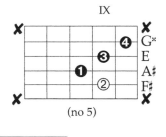

F#13♭9

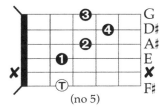
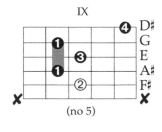

F#7+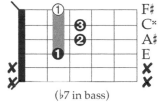

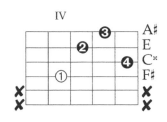

(♭7 in bass)

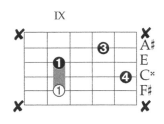

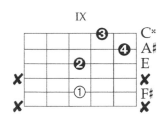

F#
Gb

F#7♭5

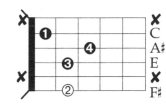

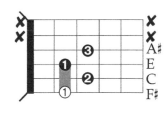

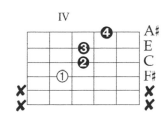

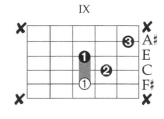

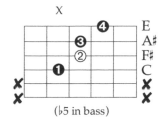

(♭5 in bass)

F#7 ♭9 #5

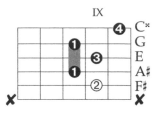

F7 #9 #5

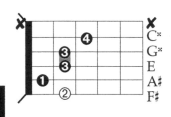

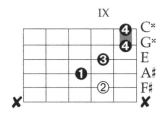

F# **G♭**

F#9#11

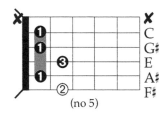

(no 5)

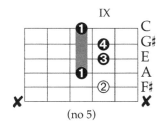

(no 5)

F#9+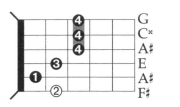

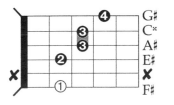

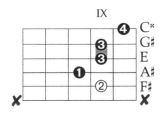

F#7sus4

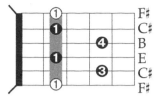
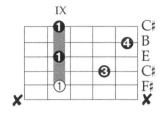
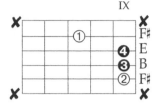
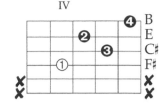
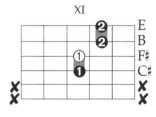

F# Gb

F#9sus4
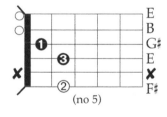
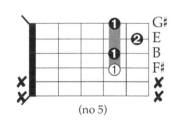
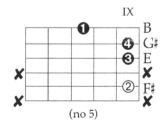
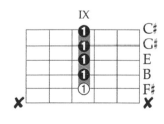

F#13sus4

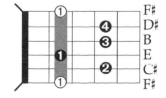
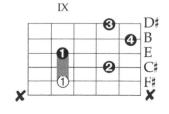

F#°

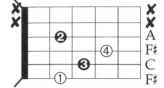

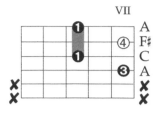

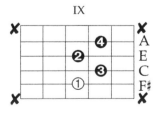

F#m7♭5

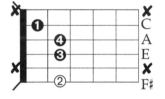

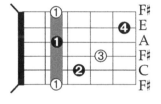

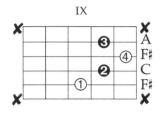

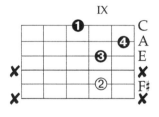

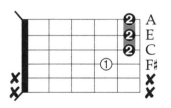

F#°7

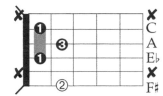

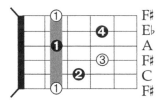

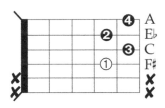

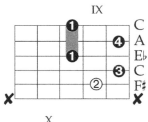

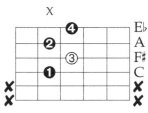

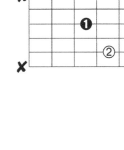

F♯+

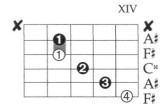

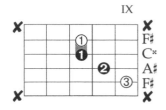

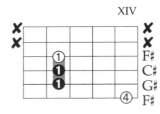

F♯sus4

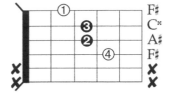

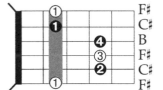

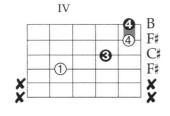

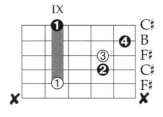

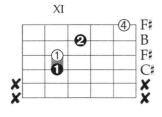

F♯sus2

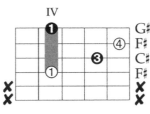

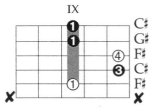

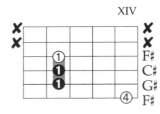

G

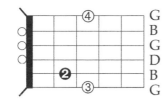

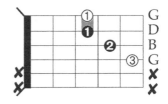

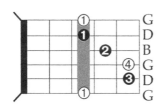

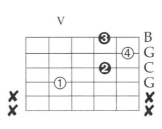

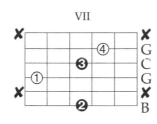

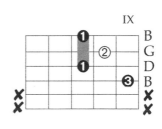

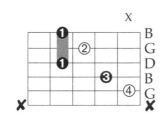

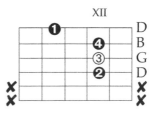

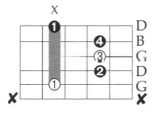

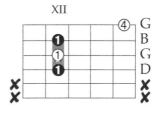

G

G6

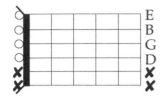
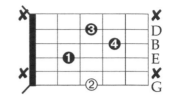

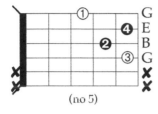
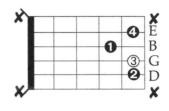

(no 5)

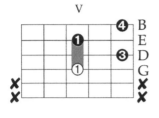
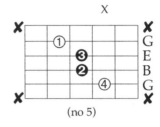

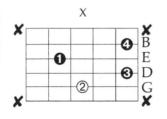
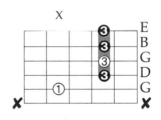

(no 5)

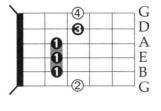
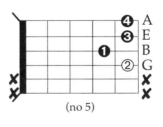

G⁶₉

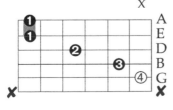
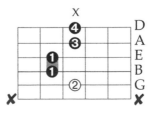

Gmaj7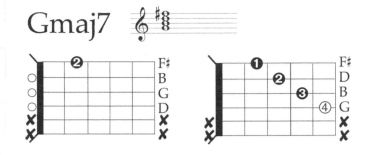

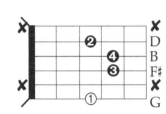

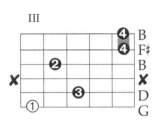

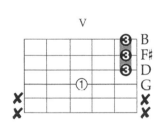

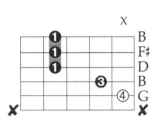

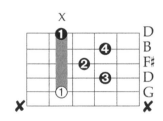

G

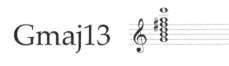

Gmaj13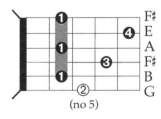

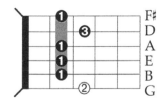

(no 5)

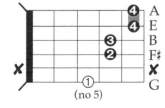

(no 5)

Gmaj9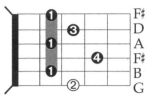

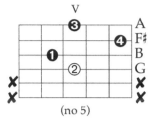
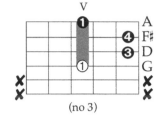

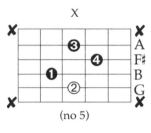
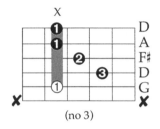

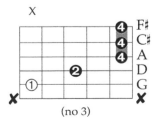

G

Gmaj9♯11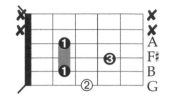

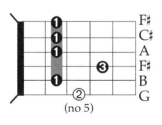
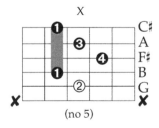

Gmaj7⁺

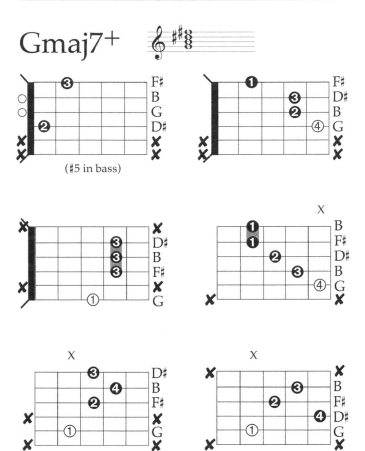

(♯5 in bass)

Gmaj7♭5

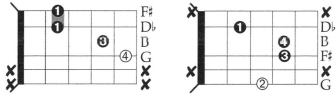

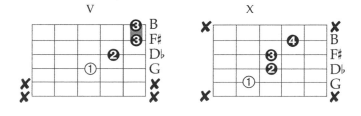

G

Gmaj13(no9)

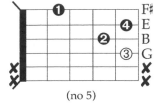
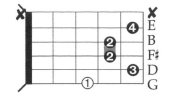

(no 5)

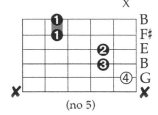
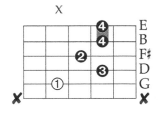

(no 5)

Gadd9

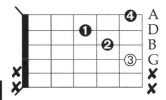
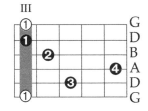

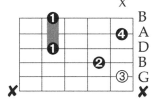
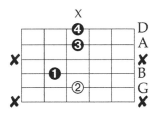

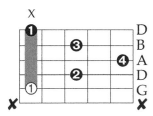

G

Gm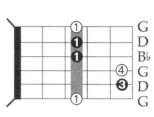

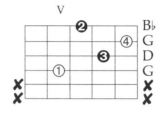

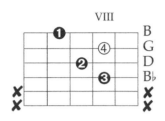

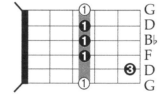

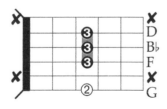

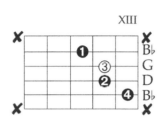

Gm7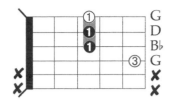

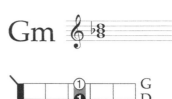

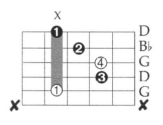

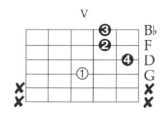

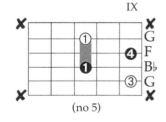

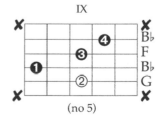

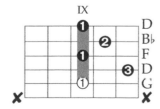

Gm6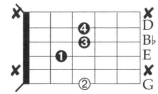

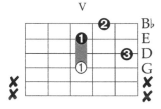

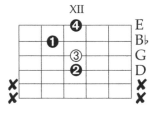

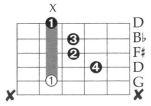

Gm(maj7)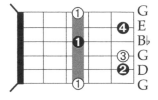

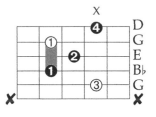

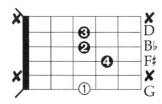 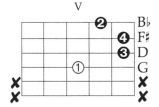

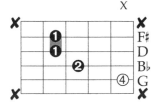 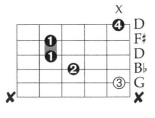

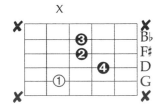

Gm add9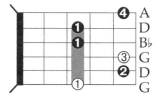

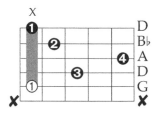

Gm9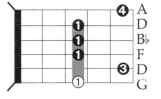

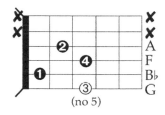
(no 5)

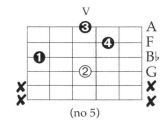
(no 5)

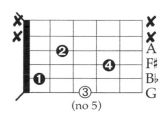

G

Gm(maj9)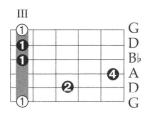

(no 5)

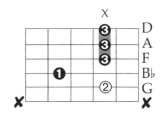

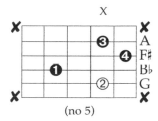
(no 5)

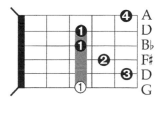

Gm⁶₉

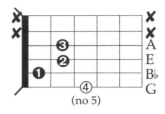

(no 5)

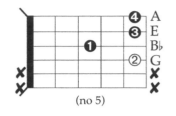

(no 5)

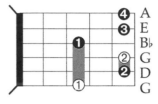

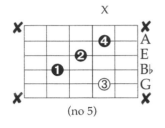

(no 5)

Gm11(no9)

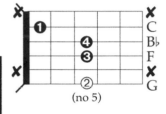

(no 5)

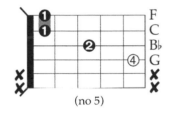

(no 5)

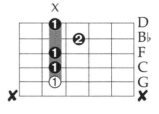

Gm11

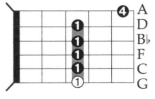

G7

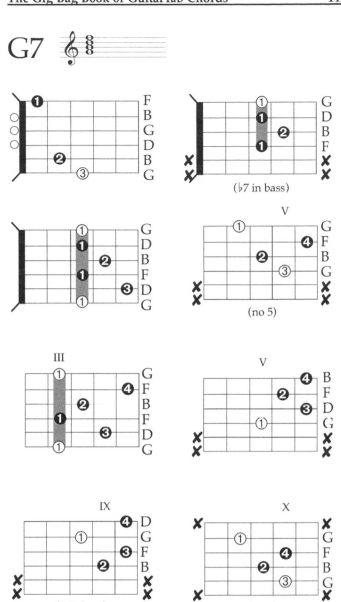

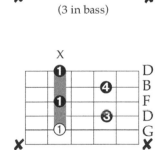

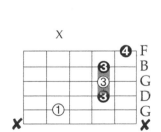

(♭7 in bass)

V
(no 5)

III

V

IX
(3 in bass)

X
(no 5)

X

X

G

G9

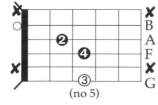

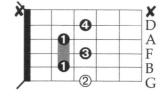

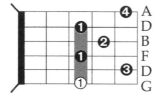

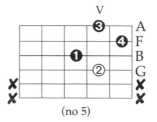

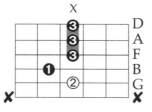

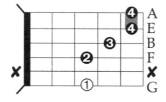

G13

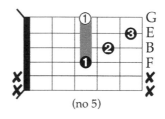

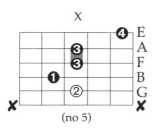

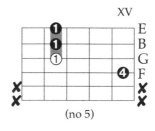

G7♭9

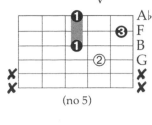

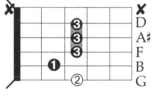

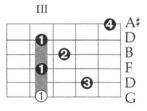

G7♯9

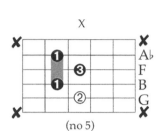

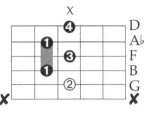

G

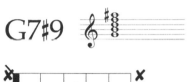

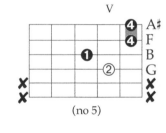

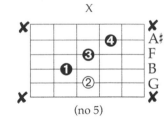

G13♭9

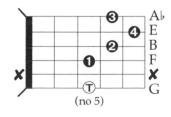

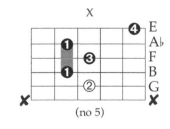

G7+

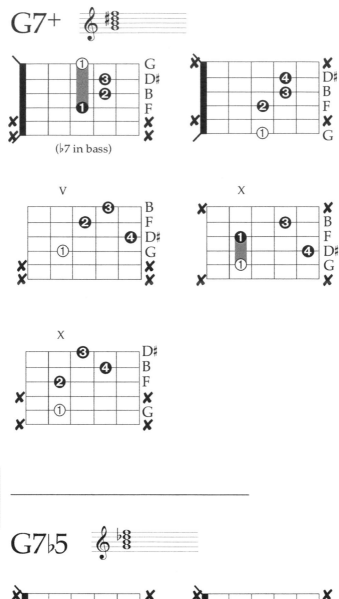

(♭7 in bass)

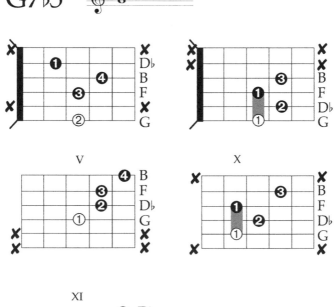

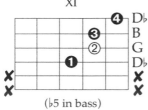

G

G7♭5

(♭5 in bass)

G7$^{\flat 9}_{\sharp 5}$

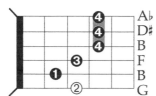 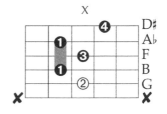

G7$^{\sharp 9}_{\sharp 5}$

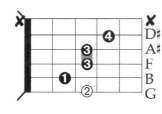 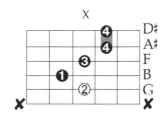

G9$\sharp$11

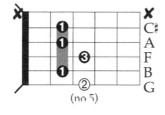 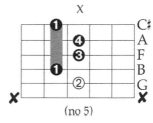

G

G9+

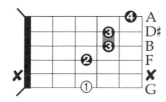 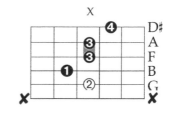

G7sus4

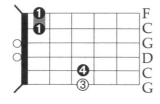

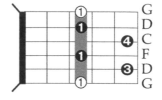

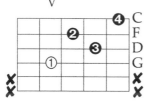

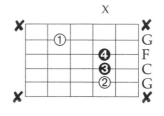

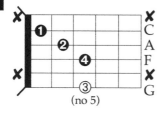

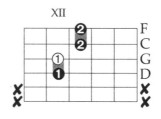

G9sus4

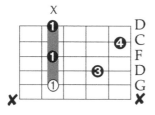

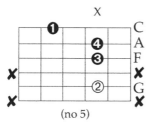

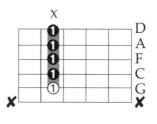

G13sus4

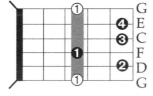

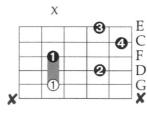

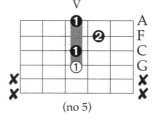

G°

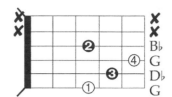

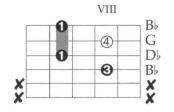

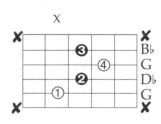

Gm7♭5

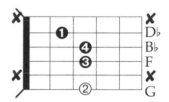

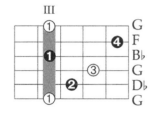

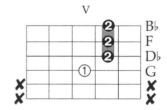

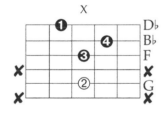

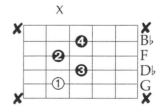

G

G°7

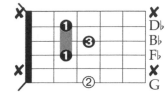

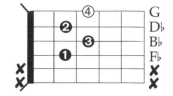

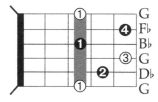

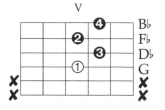

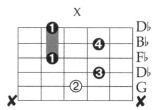

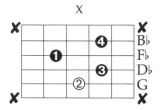

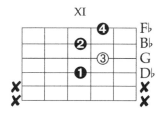

G+

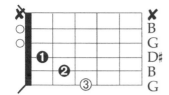

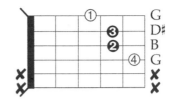

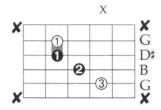

Gsus4

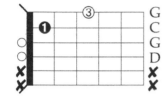

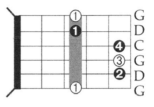

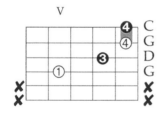

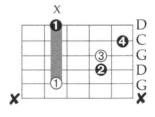

G

Gsus2

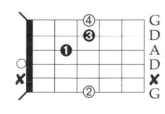

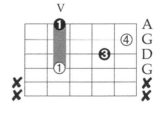

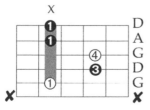

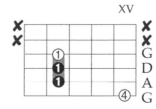

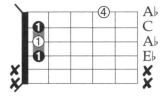

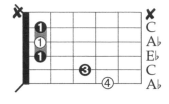

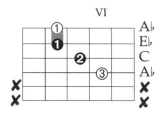

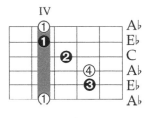

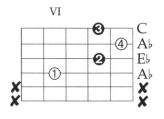

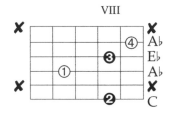

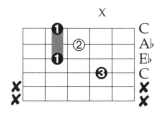

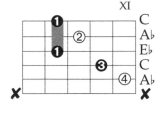

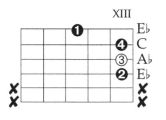

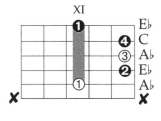

A♭
G♯

A♭6

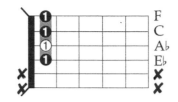

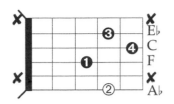

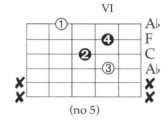

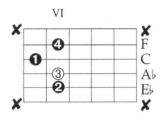

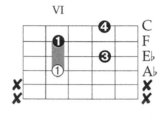

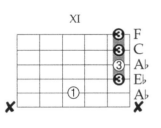

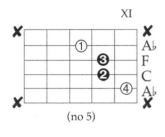

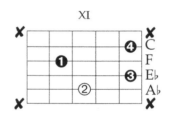

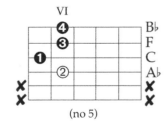

A♭ ⁶⁄₉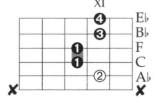

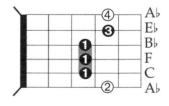

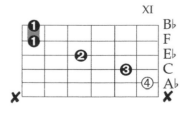

A♭maj7

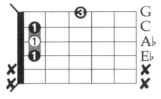
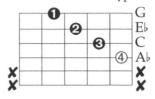
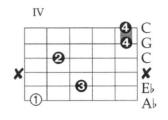
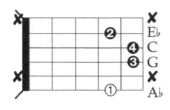
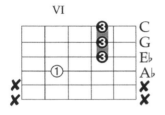
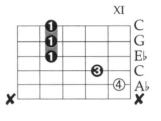
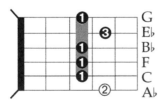
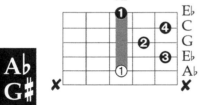

A♭ / G♯

A♭maj13

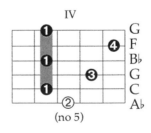
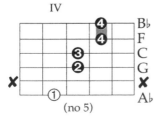

Abmaj9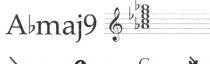

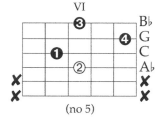

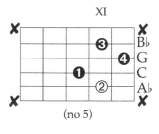

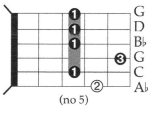

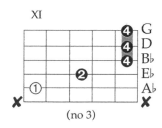

Abmaj9♯11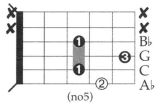

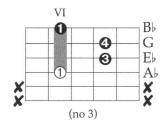

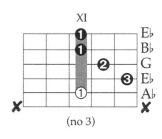

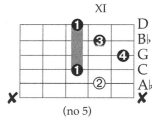

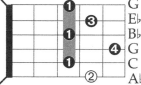

A♭maj7+

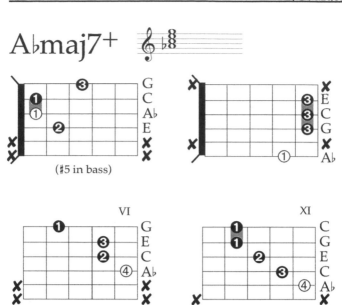

(♯5 in bass)

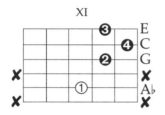

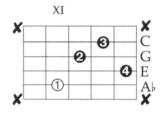

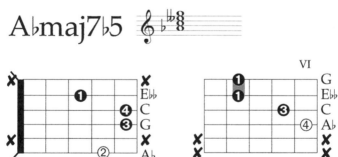

A♭maj7♭5

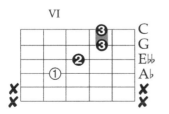

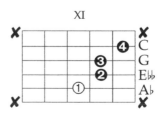

A♭maj13(no9)

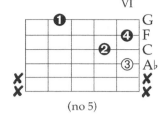

VI

G
F
C
A♭

(no 5)

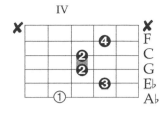

IV

F
C
G
E♭
A♭

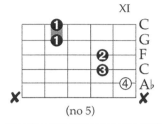

XI

C
G
F
C
A♭

(no 5)

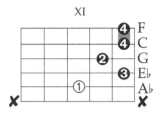

XI

F
C
G
E♭
A♭

A♭add9

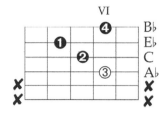

VI

B♭
E♭
C
A♭

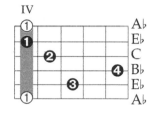

IV

A♭
E♭
C
B♭
E♭
A♭

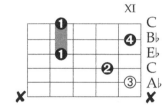

XI

C
B♭
E♭
C
A♭

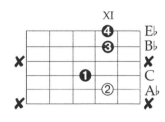

XI

E♭
B♭
C
A♭

A♭
G♯

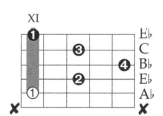

XI

E♭
C
B♭
E♭
A♭

A♭m

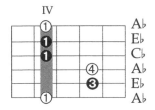

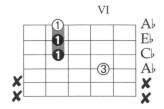

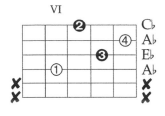

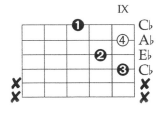

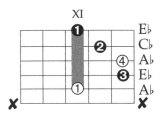

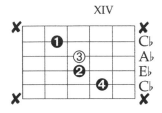

A♭m7

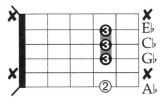

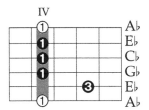

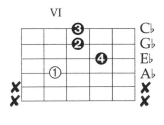

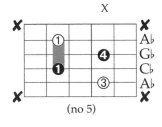

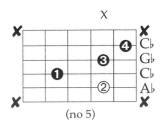

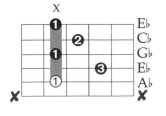

A♭m6

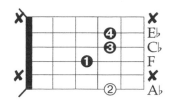

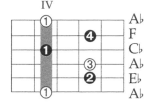

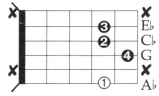

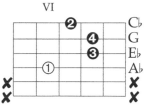

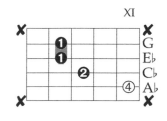

A♭m(maj7)

A♭
G#

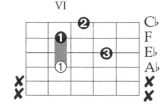

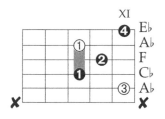

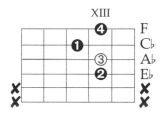

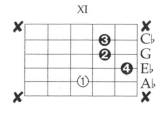

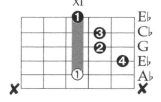

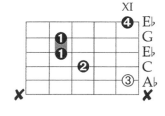

A♭m add9

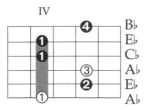

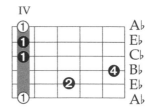

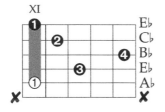

A♭m9

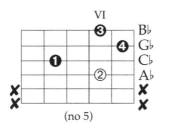

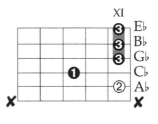

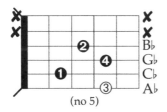

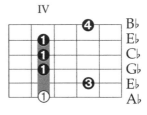

A♭m(maj9)

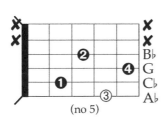

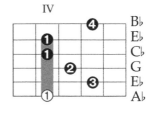

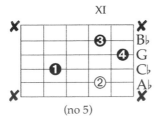

A♭m$^6_9$

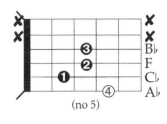

(no 5)

VI

(no 5)

IV

XI

(no 5)

A♭m11(no9)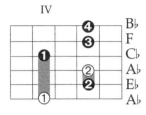

(no 5)

VI

(no 5)

XI

A♭m11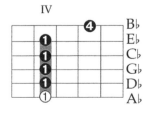

IV

A♭
G♯

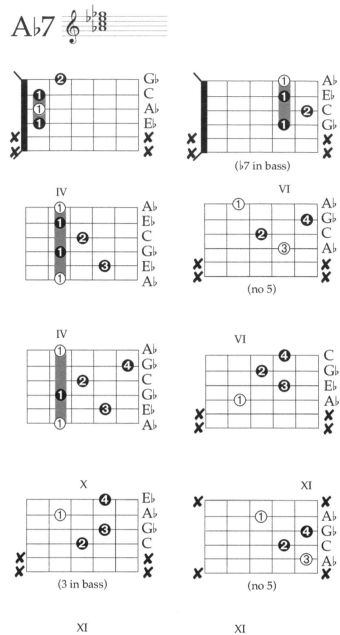

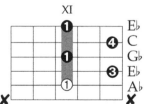

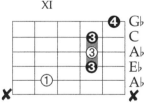

A♭9

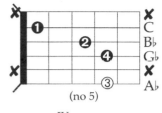

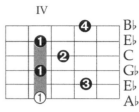

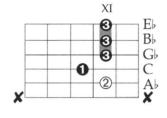

A♭13

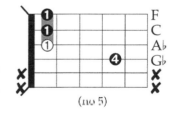

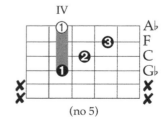

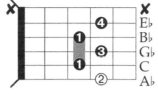

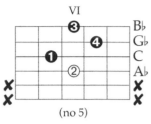

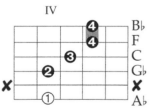

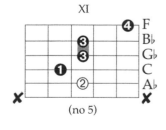

A♭
G♯

Ab7b9

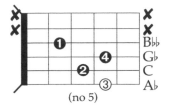

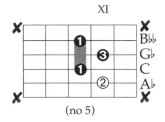
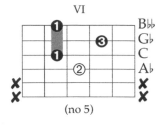

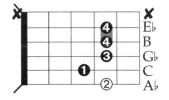
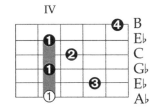

Ab7#9

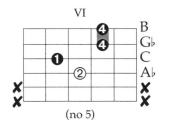
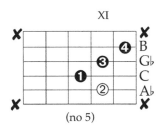

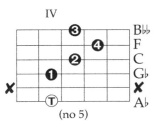
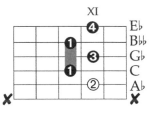

Ab13b9
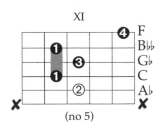

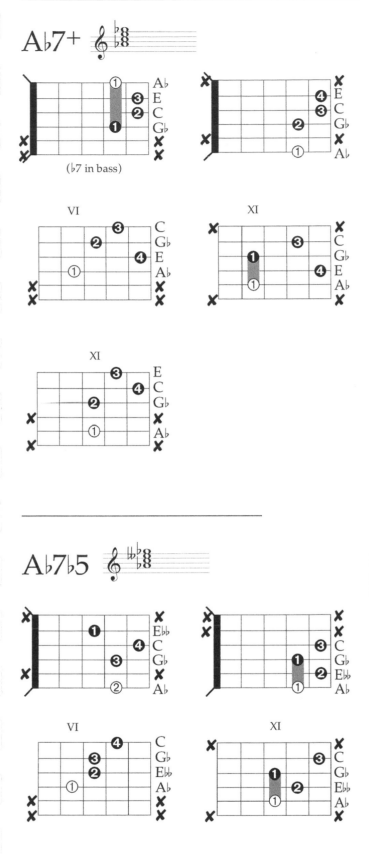

Ab7+

Ab7b5

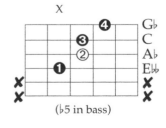

A♭7♯5♭9

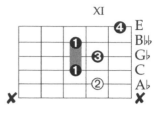

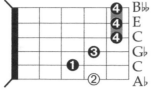

A♭7♯5#9

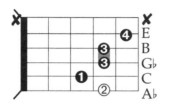

A♭
G♯

A♭9♯11

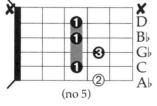

(no 5)   (no 5)

A♭9+

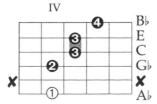

A♭7sus4

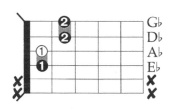

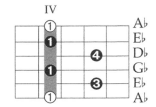

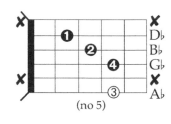

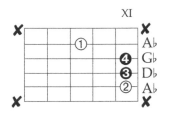

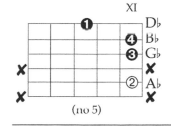

A♭9sus4

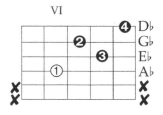

(no 5)

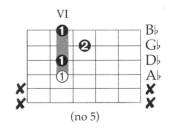

(no 5)

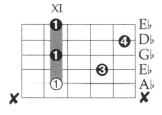

(no 5)

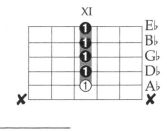

A♭13sus4

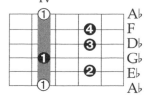

A♭
G#

A♭°

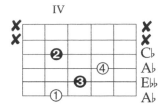

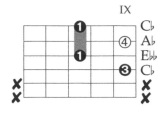

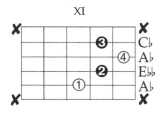

A♭m7♭5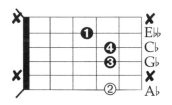

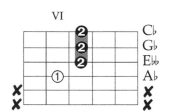

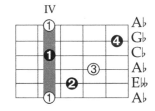

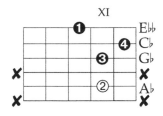

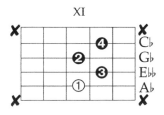

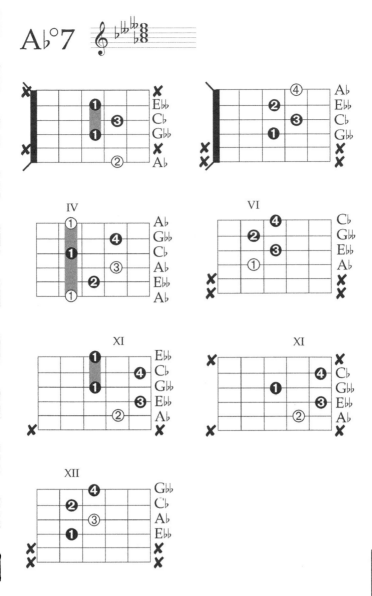

A♭+

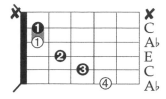
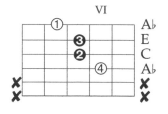
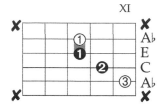

A♭sus4

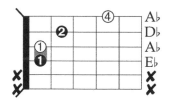
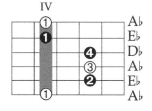
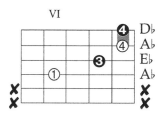
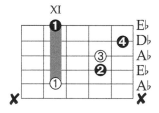

A♭sus2

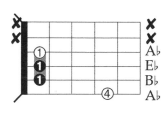
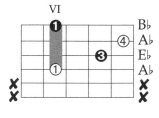
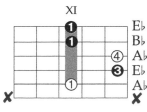

A

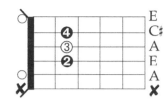

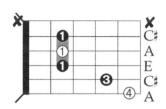

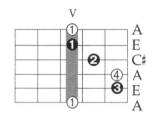

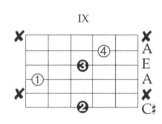

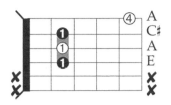

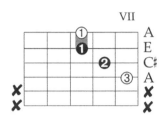

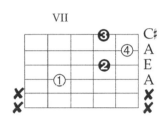

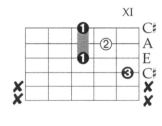

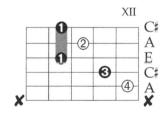

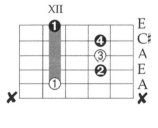

A6

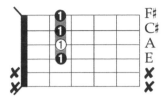

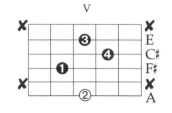

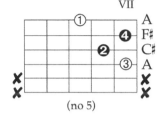

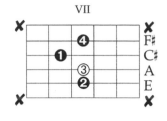

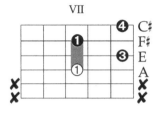

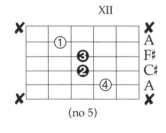

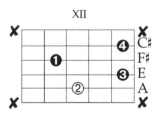

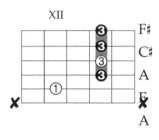

A

A$^6_9$

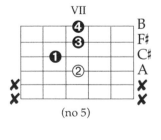

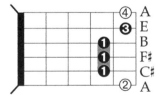

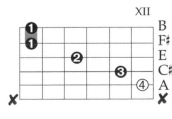

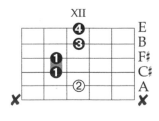

Amaj7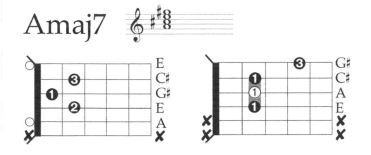

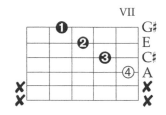

E
C#
G#
E
A

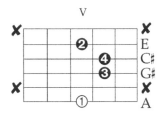

G#
C#
A
E

VII

G#
E
C#
A

V

E
C#
G#
A

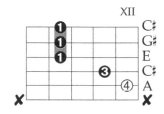

V

C#
G#
C#
E
A

VII

C#
G#
E
A

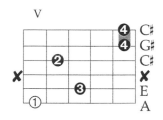

XII

C#
G#
E
C#
A

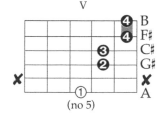

Amaj13

A

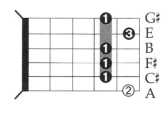

G#
E
B
F#
C#
A

V

G#
F#
B
G#
C#
A

(no 5)

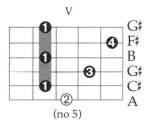

V

B
F#
C#
G#
A

(no 5)

Amaj9

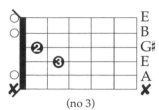
(no 3)

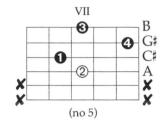

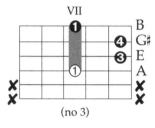

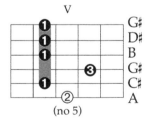
(no 5)

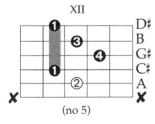
(no 3)

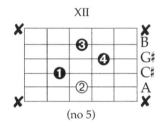
(no 5)

Amaj9♯11

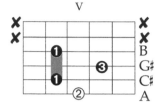
(no 3)

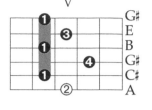
(no 5)

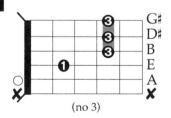
(no 5)

Amaj7+

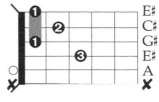

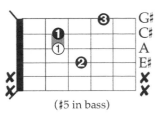

(♯5 in bass)

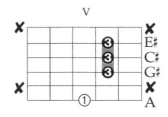

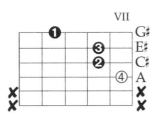

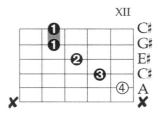

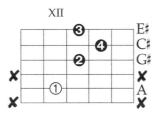

Amaj7♭5

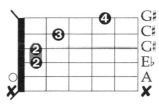

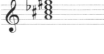

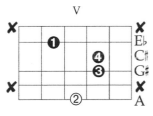

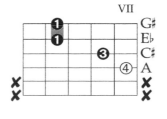

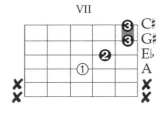

A

Amaj13(no9)

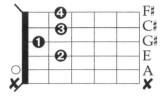

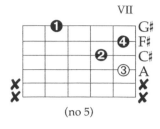

(no 5)

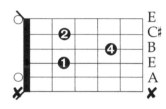

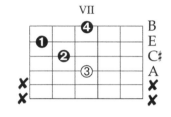

(no 5)

Aadd9

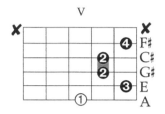

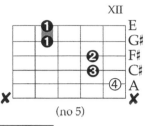

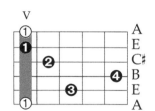

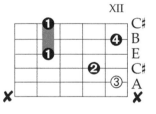

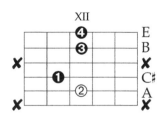

Am

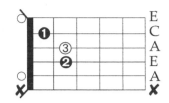

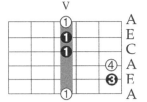

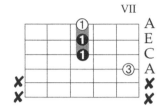

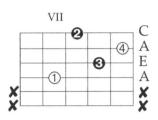

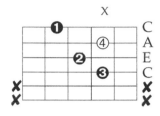

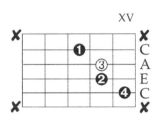

Am7

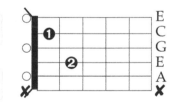

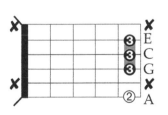

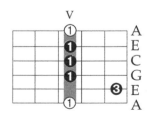

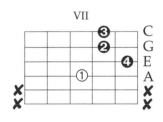

(no 5)

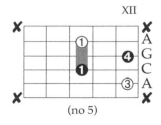

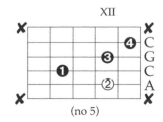

(no 5)   (no 5)

A

Am6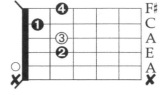

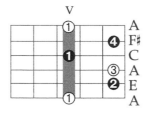
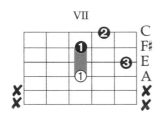

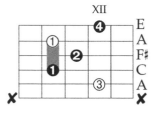
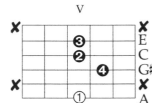

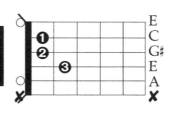

Am(maj7)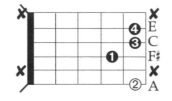

A

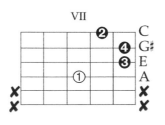
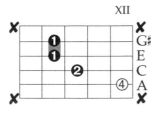

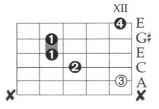
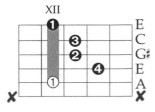

Am add9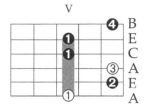

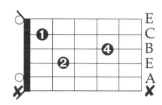

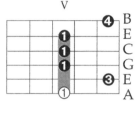

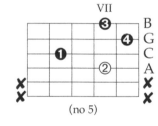

Am9

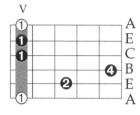

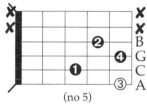

(no 5)

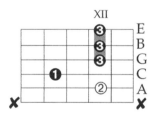

(no 5)

Am(maj9)

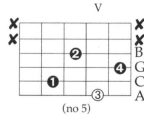

(no 5)

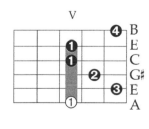

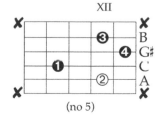

(no 5)

A

Am$_9^6$

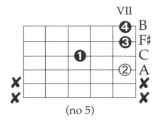

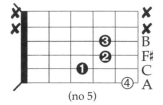

(no 5)

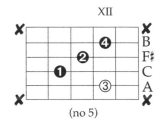

(no 5)

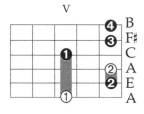

Am11(no9)

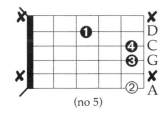

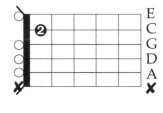

(no 5)

A

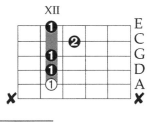

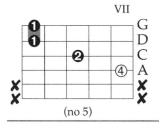

(no 5)

Am11

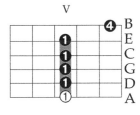

A7

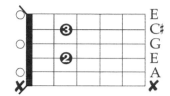

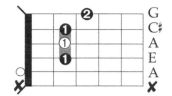

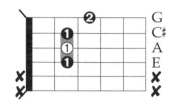

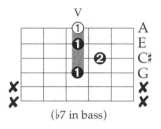

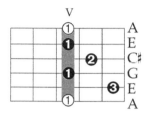

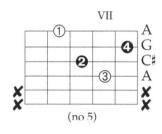
(♭7 in bass)

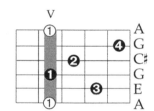

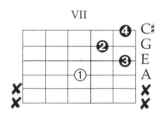
(no 5)

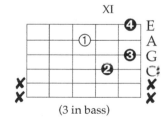

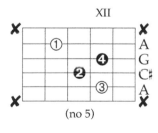

(3 in bass)

(no 5)

A

A9

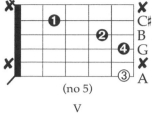

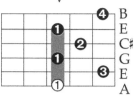

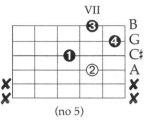

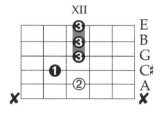

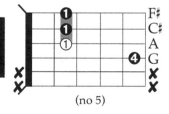

A13

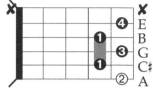

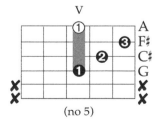

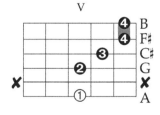

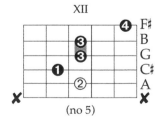

A7♭9

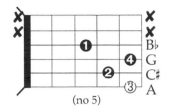
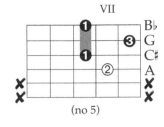

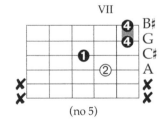
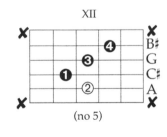

A7♯9

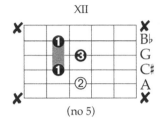
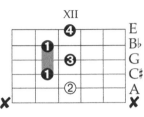

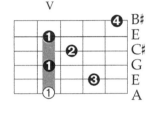

A13♭9

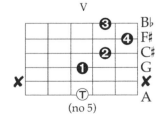
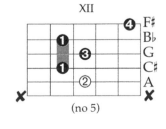

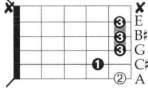

A

A7⁺

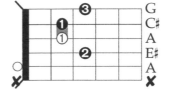

G
C#
A
E#
A

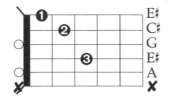

E#
C#
G
E#
A

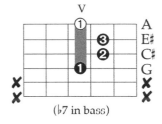

V

A
E#
C#
G

(♭7 in bass)

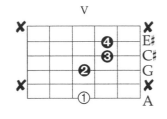

V

E#
C#
G
A

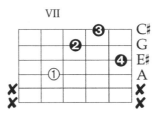

VII

C#
G
E#
A

A7♭5

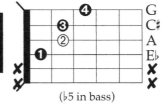

G
C#
A
E♭

(♭5 in bass)

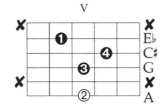

V

E♭
C#
G
A

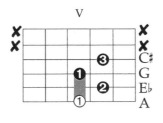

V

C#
G
E♭
A

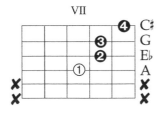

VII

C#
G
E♭
A

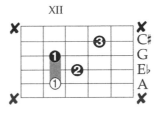

XII

C#
G
E♭
A

A

A7♭9♯5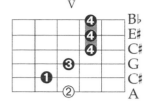

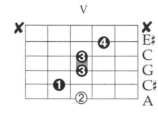

A7♯9♯5

A9♯11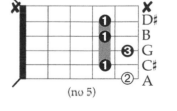

A9+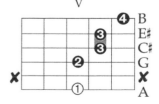

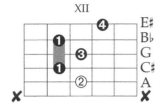
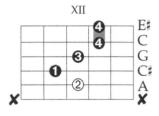
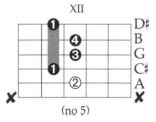
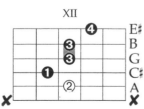

A

A7sus4

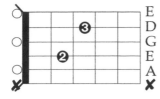

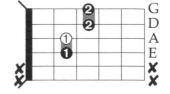

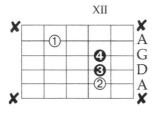

A9sus4

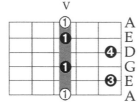

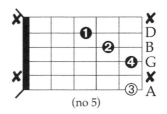

(no 5)

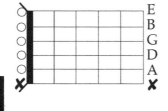

(no 5)

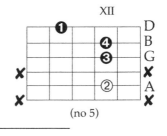

(no 5)

A13sus4

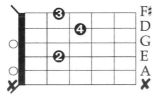

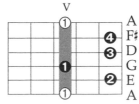

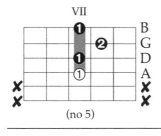

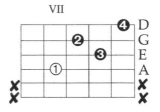

A°

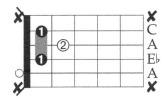

V

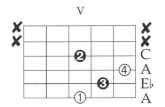

X

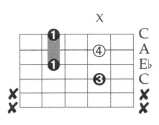

Am7♭5

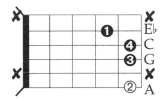

V

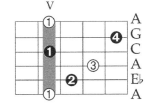

VII

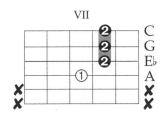

XII

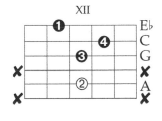

XII

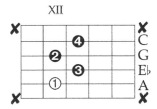

A

A°7

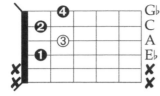

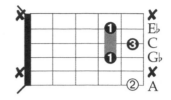

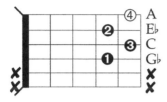

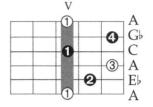

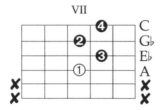

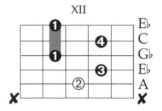

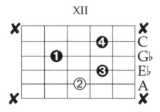

A+

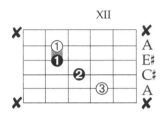
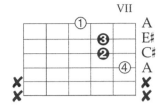

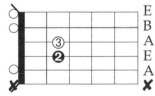

Asus4

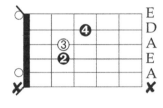
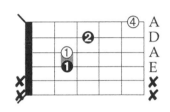

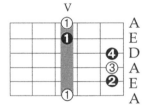
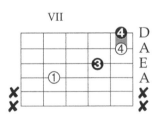

Asus2

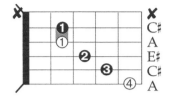

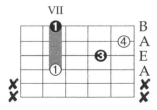
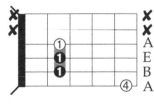

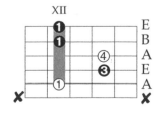

A

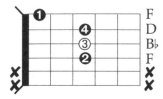

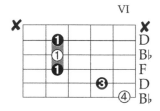

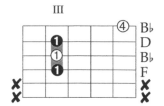

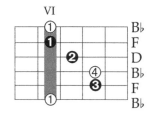

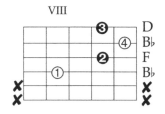

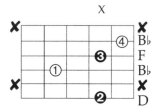

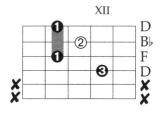

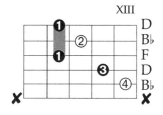

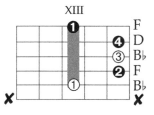

Bb6

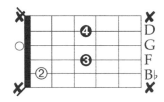

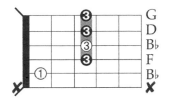

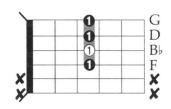

VI

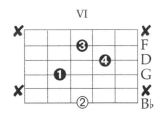

VIII

(no 5)

VIII

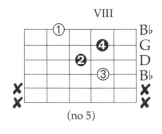

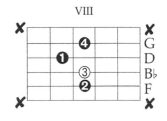

VIII

XIII

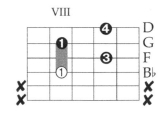

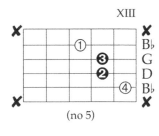

(no 5)

Bb 6/9

VI

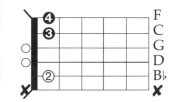

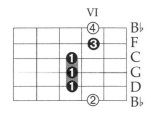

VIII

XIII

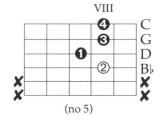

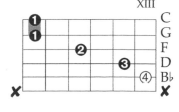

(no 5)

Bb
A#

B♭maj7

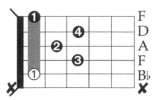

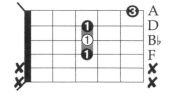

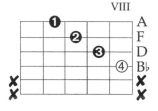

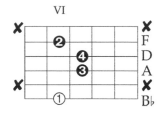

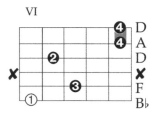

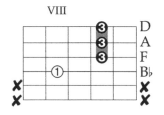

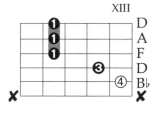

B♭maj13

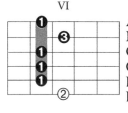

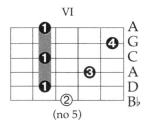

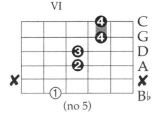

B♭maj9

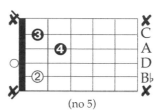
(no 5)

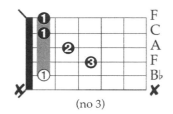
(no 3)

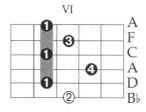

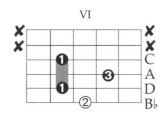

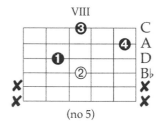
(no 5)

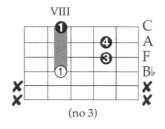
(no 3)

B♭maj9♯11

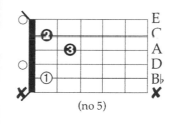
(no 5)

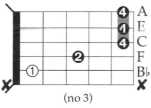
(no 3)

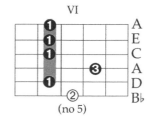
(no 5)

B♭maj7+

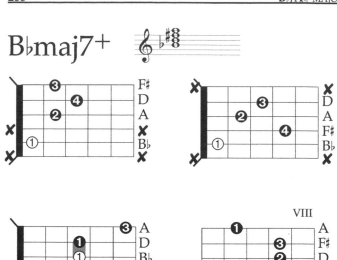

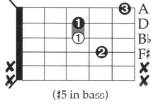

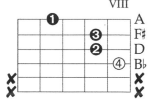

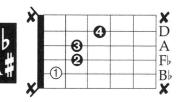

(♯5 in bass)

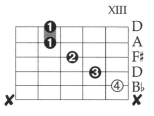

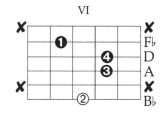

B♭maj7♭5

B♭
A♯

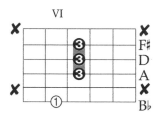

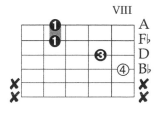

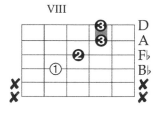

Bbmaj13(no9)

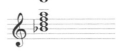

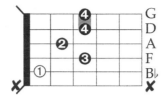

G
D
A
F
Bb

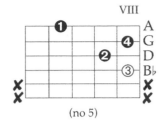

VIII

A
G
D
Bb

(no 5)

VI

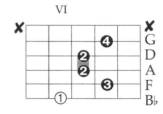

G
D
A
F
Bb

XIII

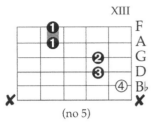

F
A
G
D
Bb

(no 5)

Bbadd9

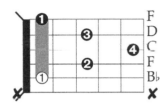

F
C

D
Bb

F
D
C
F
Bb

VIII

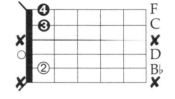

C
F
D
Bb

VI

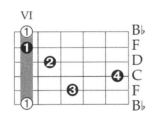

Bb
F
D
C
F
Bb

XIII

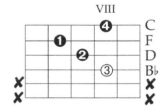

D
C
F
D
Bb

Bb
A#

Bbm

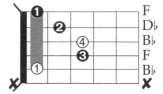

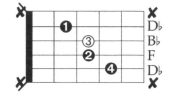

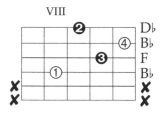

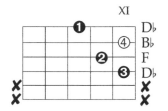

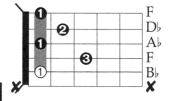

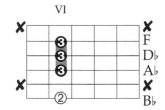

Bbm7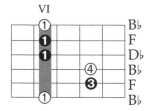

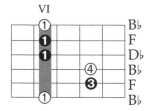

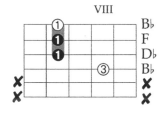

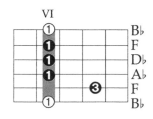

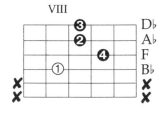

Bb
A#

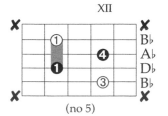

(no 5)

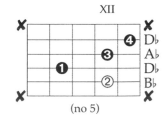

(no 5)

B♭m6

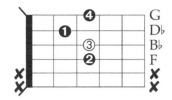
G
D♭
B♭
F

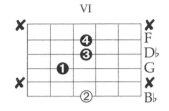
F
D♭
G
B♭

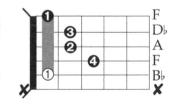
B♭
G
D♭
B♭
F
B♭

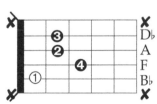
D♭
G
F
B♭

F
B♭
G
D♭
B♭

B♭m(maj7)

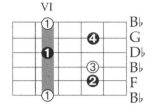
F
D♭
A
F
B♭

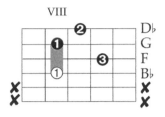
D♭
A
F
B♭

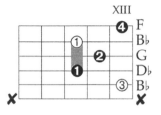
F
D♭
A
B♭

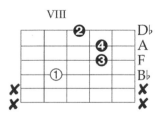
D♭
A
F
B♭

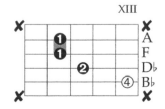
A
F
D♭
B♭

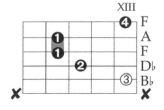
F
A
F
D♭
B♭

B♭
A#

B♭m add9
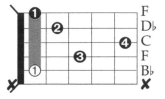
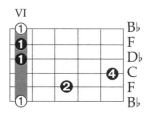

B♭m9

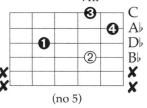
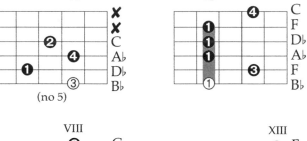

B♭m(maj9)

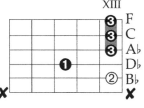
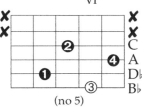
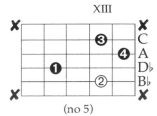
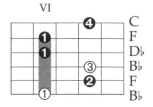

Bbm$^6_9$

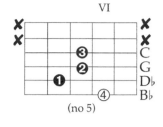

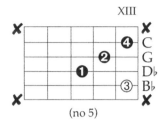

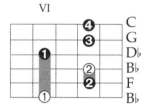

Bbm11(no9)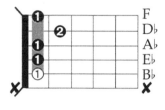

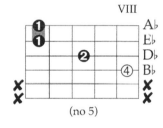

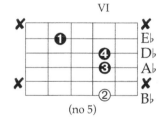

Bbm11

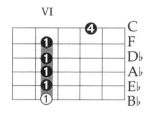

Bb7

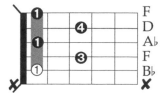

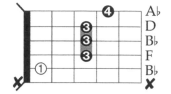

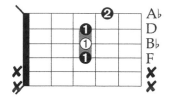

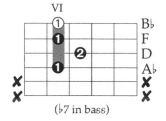

(b7 in bass)

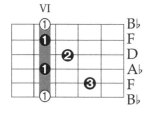

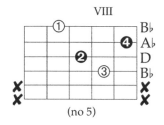

(no 5)

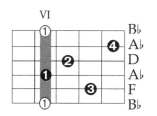

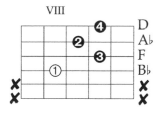

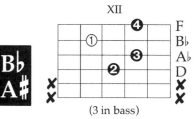

(3 in bass)

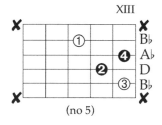

(no 5)

Bb
A♯

B♭9

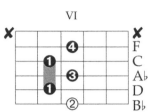
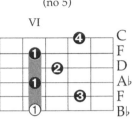

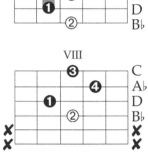

B♭13

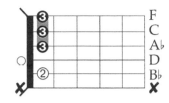

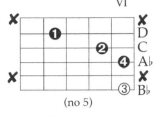

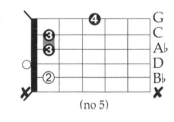
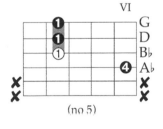

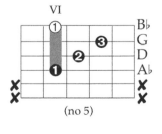
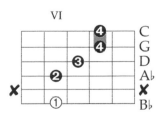

Bb7b9

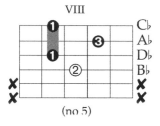

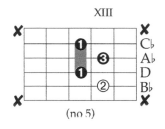

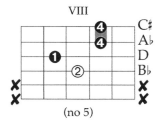

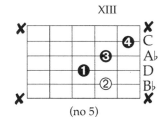

Bb7#9

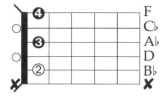

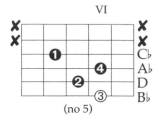

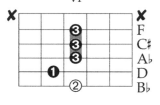

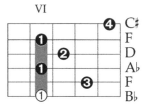

Bb / A#

Bb13b9

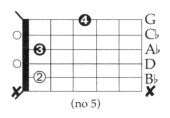

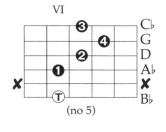

B♭7+

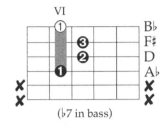

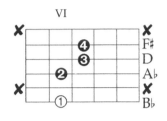

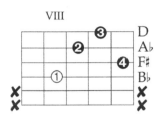

(♭7 in bass)

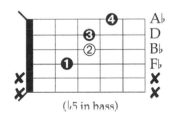

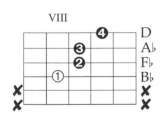

B♭7♭5

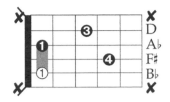

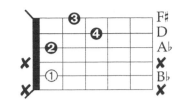

(♭5 in bass)

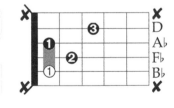

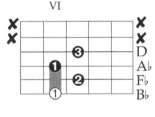

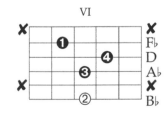

B♭
A#

B♭7 ♭9 ♯5

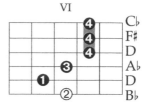

Bb
A♯

B♭7 ♯9 ♯5

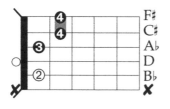 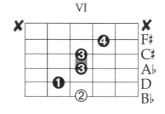

B♭9♯11

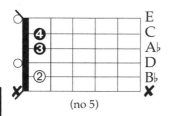 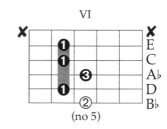

(no 5)   (no 5)

B♭9+

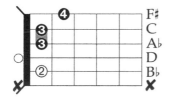 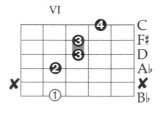

Bb7sus4

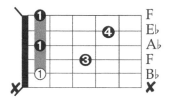

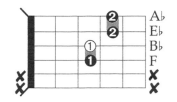

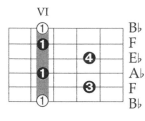

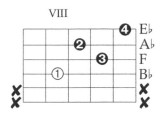

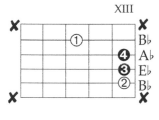

Bb9sus4

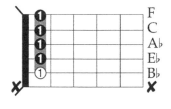

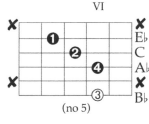

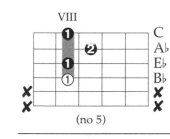

(no 5)

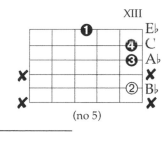

(no 5)

Bb13sus4

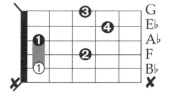

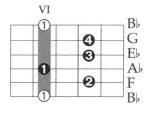

Bb
A#

B♭°

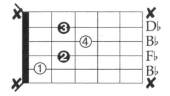

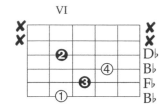

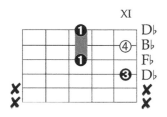

B♭m7♭5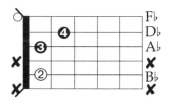

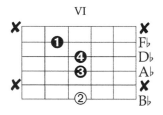

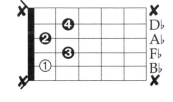

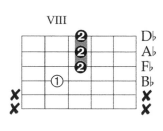

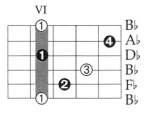

B♭°7

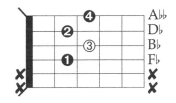

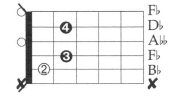

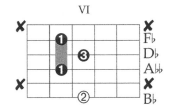

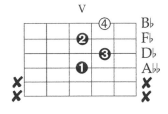

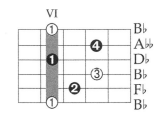

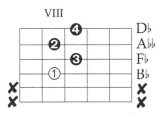

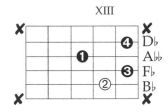

Bb+

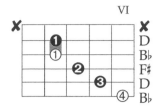 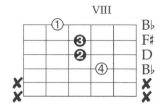

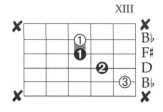

Bbsus4

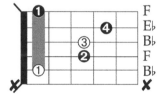 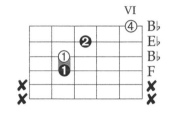

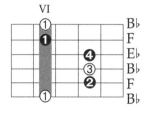 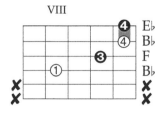

Bbsus2

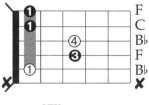 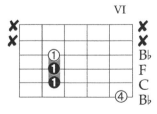

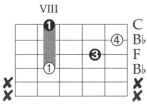

B

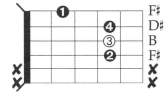

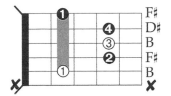

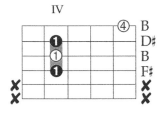

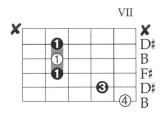

IV   VII

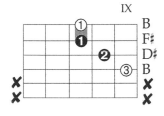

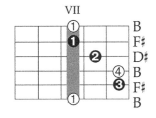

IX   VII

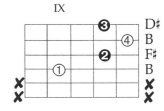

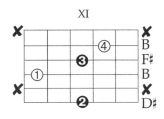

IX   XI

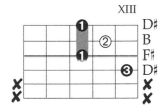

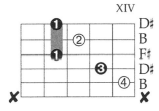

XIII   XIV

B

B6

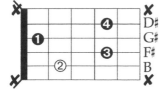

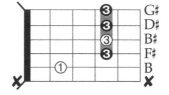

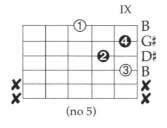

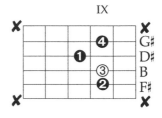

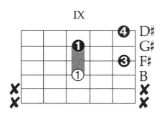

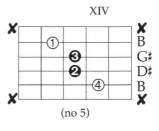

(no 5)

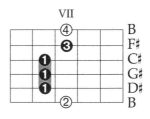

(no 5)

B$^6_9$

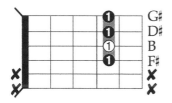

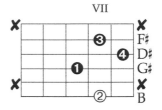

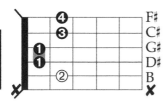

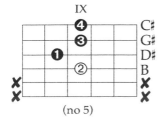

(no 5)

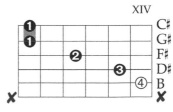

B

Bmaj7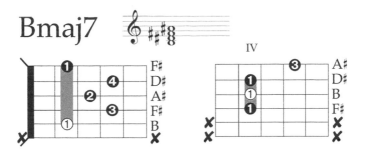

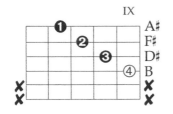

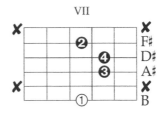

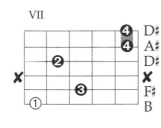

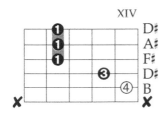

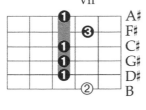

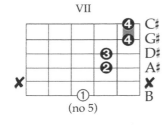

Bmaj13

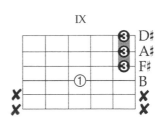

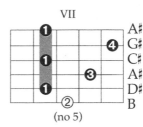

(no 5)

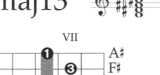

(no 5)

B

Bmaj9

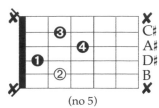

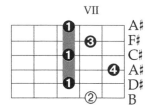 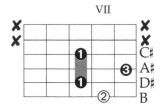

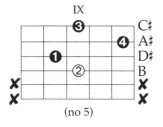 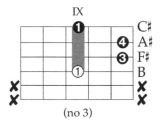

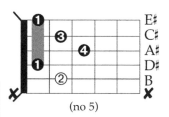 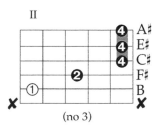

Bmaj9#11

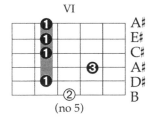 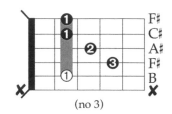

Bmaj7+

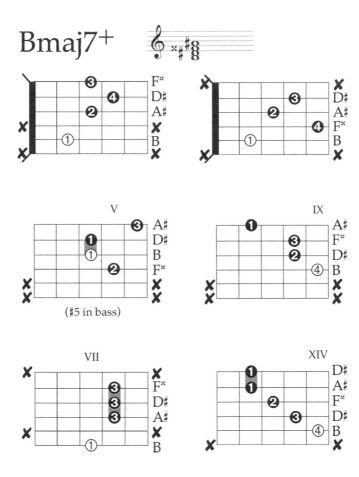

(♯5 in bass)

Bmaj7♭5

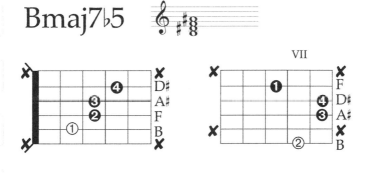

B

Bmaj13(no9)

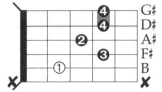

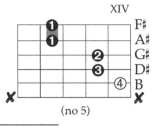

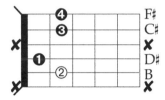

(no 5)

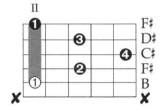

(no 5)

Badd9

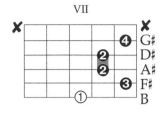

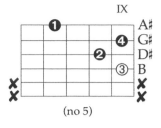

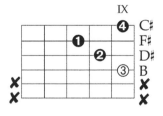

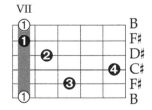

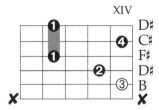

B

Bm

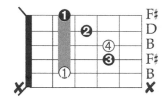

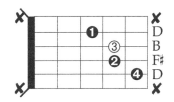

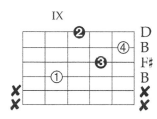

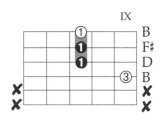

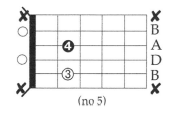

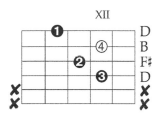

Bm7

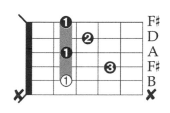

(no 5)

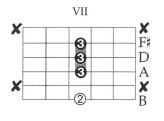

(no 5)

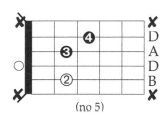

B

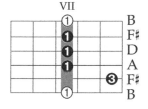

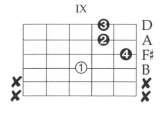

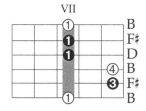

Bm6

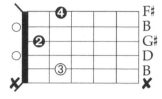

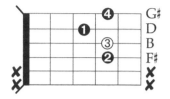

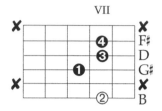

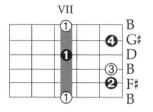

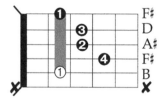

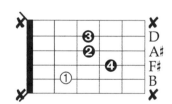

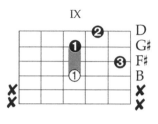

Bm(maj7)

B

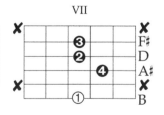

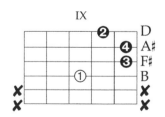

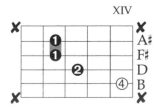

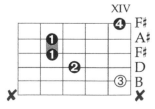

Bm add9

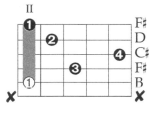

F#
D
C#
F#
B

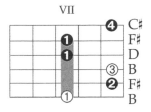

C#
F#
D
B
F#
B

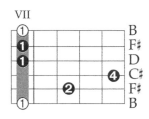

B
F#
D
C#
F#
B

Bm9

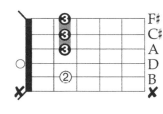

F#
C#
A
D
B

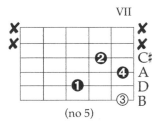

C#
A
D
B

(no 5)

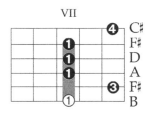

C#
F#
D
A
F#
B

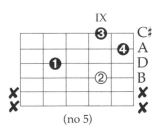

C#
A
D
B

(no 5)

Bm(maj9)

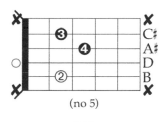

C#
A#
D
B

(no 5)

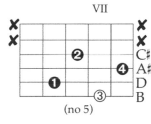

C#
A#
D
B

(no 5)

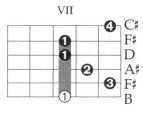

C#
F#
D
A#
F#
B

B

Bm⁶₉

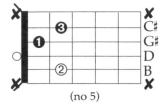

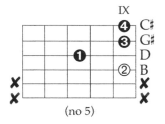

Bm11(no9)

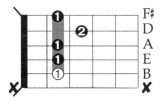

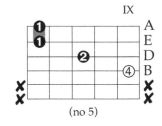

Bm11

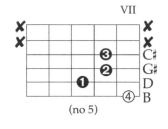

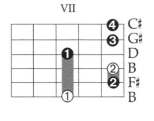

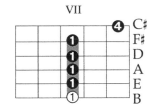

B7

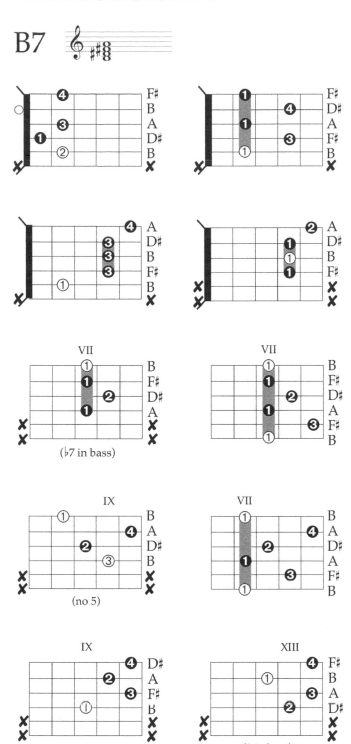

B9

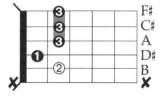

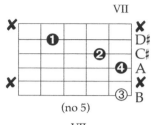

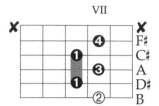

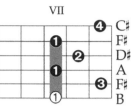

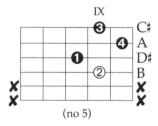

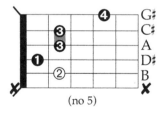

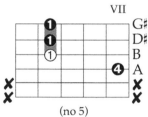

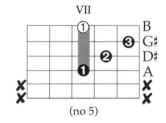

B13

B

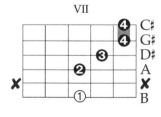

B7♭9

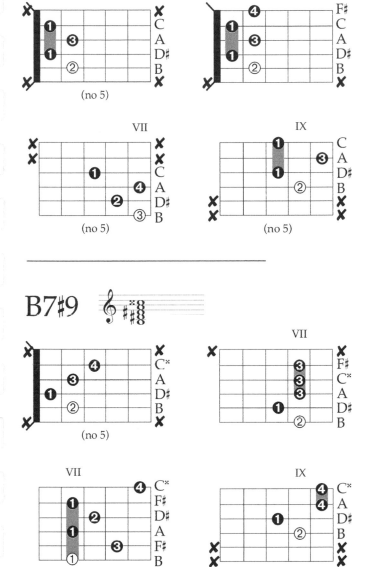

B7♯9

B13♭9

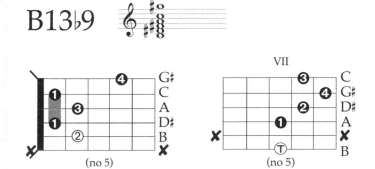

B

B7+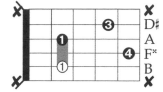

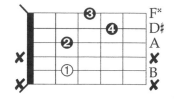

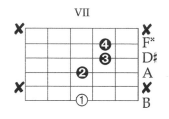

VII

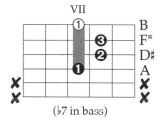

(♭7 in bass)

VII

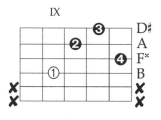

IX

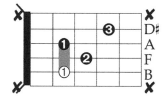

B7♭5

(♭5 in bass)

VII

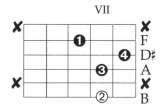

VII

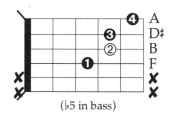

IX

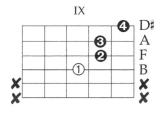

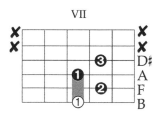

B

B7$_{\sharp5}^{\flat9}$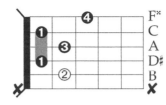

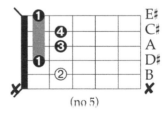

B7$_{\sharp5}^{\sharp9}$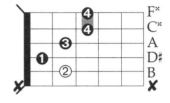

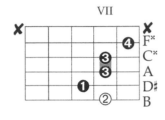

B9$\sharp$11

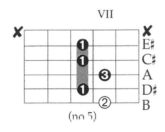

(no 5)   (no 5)

B

B9+

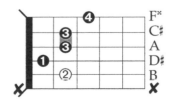

B7sus4

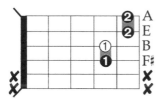

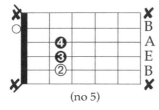

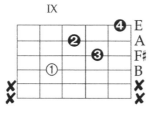

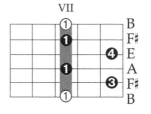

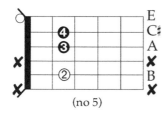

B9sus4

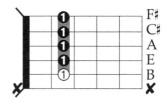

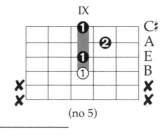

B13sus4

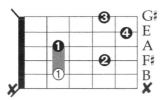

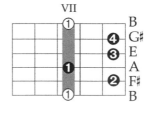

B

B°

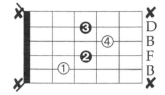

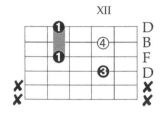

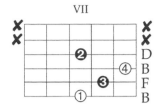

Bm7♭5

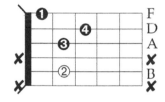

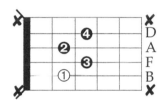

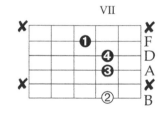

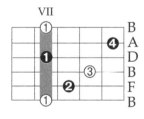

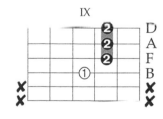

B

B°7

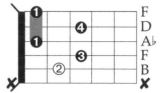

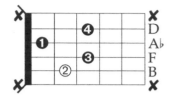

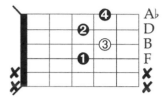

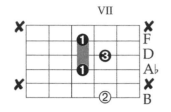

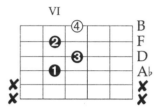

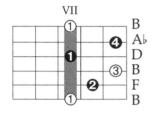

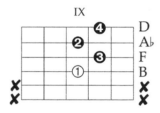

B

B+

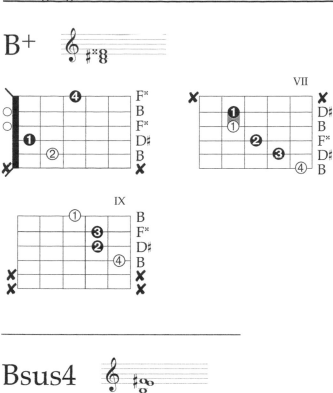

Bsus4

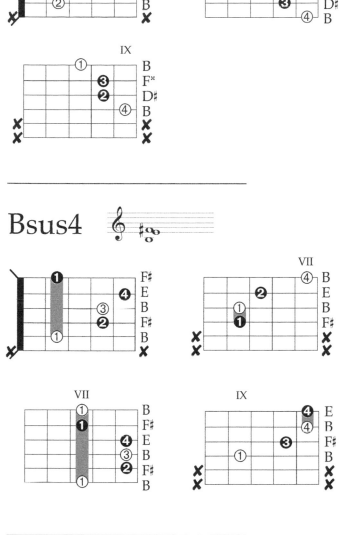

Bsus2

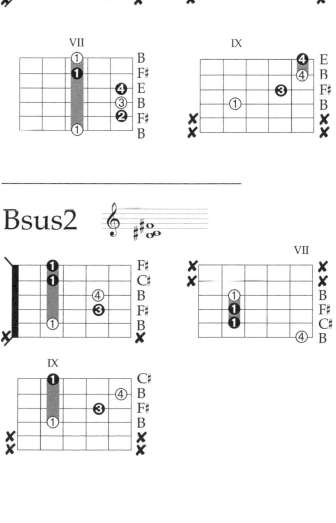

B

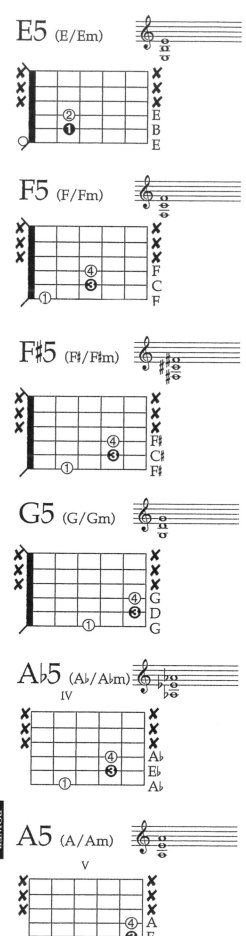

E5 (E/Em)

F5 (F/Fm)

F#5 (F#/F#m)

G5 (G/Gm)

Ab5 (Ab/Abm)

A5 (A/Am)

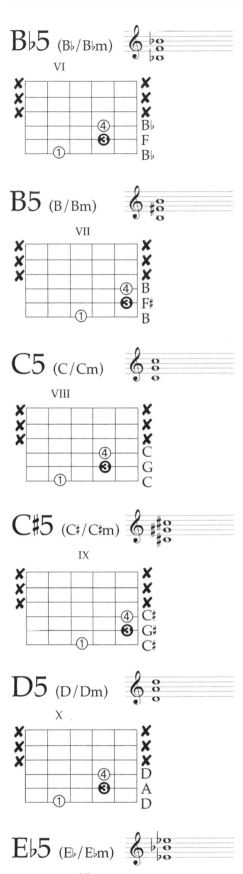

Bb5 (Bb/Bbm)

VI

Bb
F
Bb

B5 (B/Bm)

VII

B
F#
B

C5 (C/Cm)

VIII

C
G
C

C#5 (C#/C#m)

IX

C#
G#
C#

D5 (D/Dm)

X

D
A
D

Eb5 (Eb/Ebm)

XI

Eb
Bb
Eb

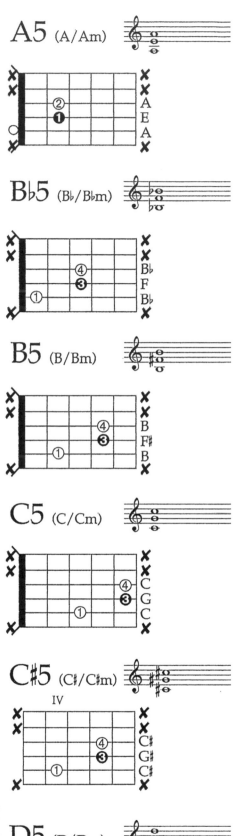

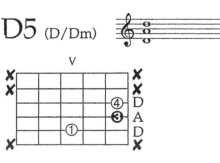

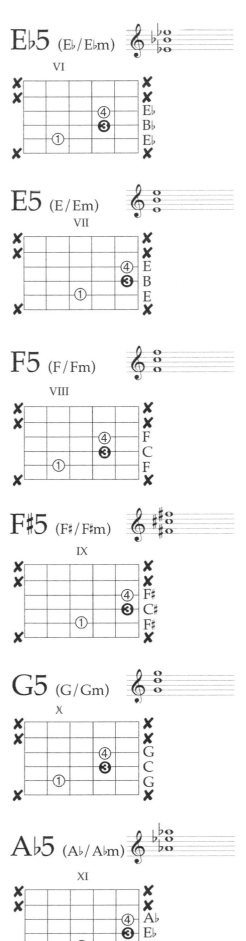

E♭5 (E♭/E♭m)

VI

E♭
B♭
E♭

E5 (E/Em)

VII

E
B
E

F5 (F/Fm)

VIII

F
C
F

F♯5 (F♯/F♯m)

IX

F♯
C♯
F♯

G5 (G/Gm)

X

G
C
G

A♭5 (A♭/A♭m)

XI

A♭
E♭
A♭

POWER
CHORDS

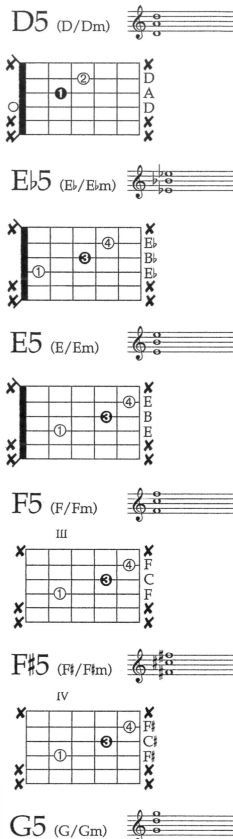

D5 (D/Dm)

Eb5 (Eb/Ebm)

E5 (E/Em)

F5 (F/Fm)

F#5 (F#/F#m)

G5 (G/Gm)

POWER
CHORDS

Ab5 (Ab / Abm)

VI

| X | | | | | X |
Ab (④)
Eb ❸
Ab ①
X
X

A5 (A / Am)

VII

| X | | | | | X |
A (④)
E ❸
A ①
X
X

Bb5 (Bb / Bbm)

VIII

| X | | | | | X |
Bb (④)
F ❸
Bb ①
X
X

B5 (B / Bm)

IX

| X | | | | | X |
B (④)
F# ❸
B ①
X
X

C5 (C / Cm)

X

| X | | | | | X |
C (④)
G ❸
C ①
X
X

C#5 (C# / C#m)

XI

| X | | | | | X |
C# (④)
G# ❸
C# ①
X
X

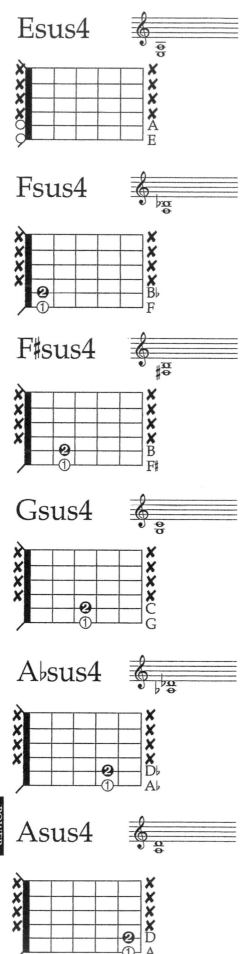

Bbsus4

Bsus4

Csus4

C#sus4

Dsus4

Ebsus4

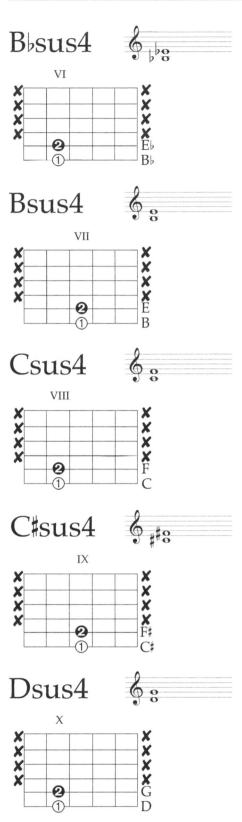

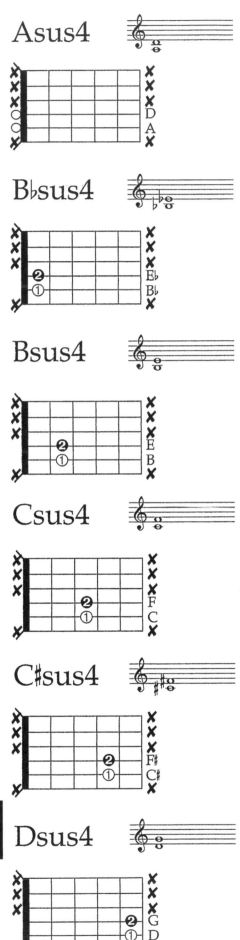

Asus4

B♭sus4

Bsus4

Csus4

C#sus4

Dsus4

POWER CHORDS

E♭sus4

Esus4

Fsus4

F♯sus4

Gsus4

A♭sus4

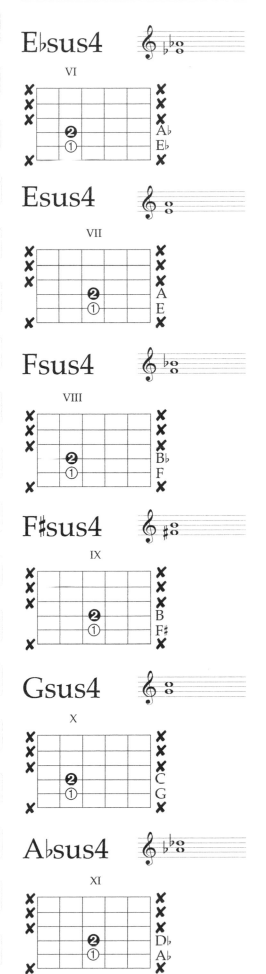

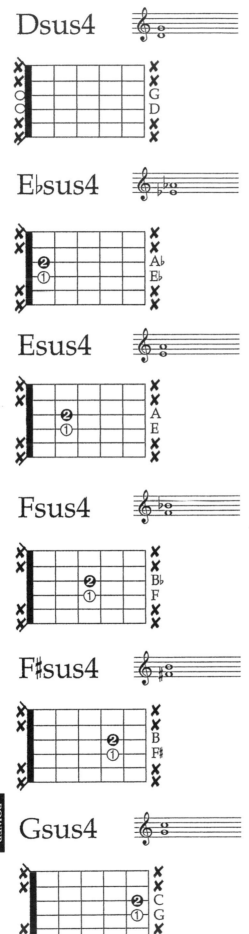

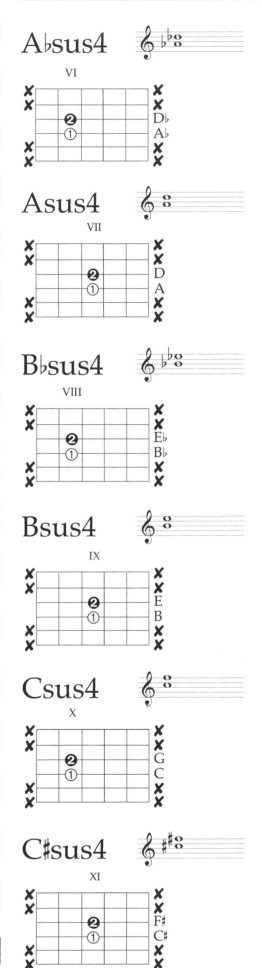

A♭sus4

Asus4

B♭sus4

Bsus4

Csus4

C♯sus4

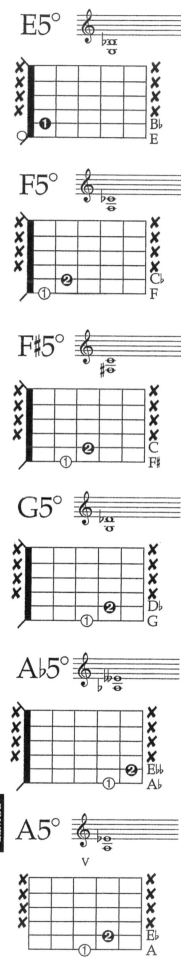

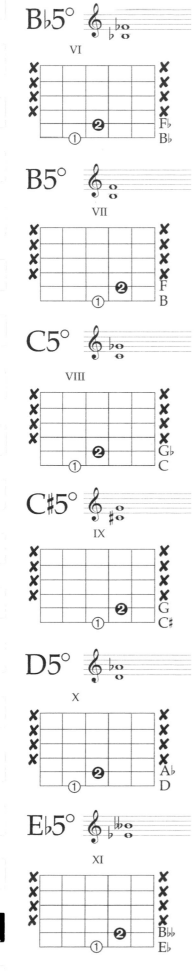

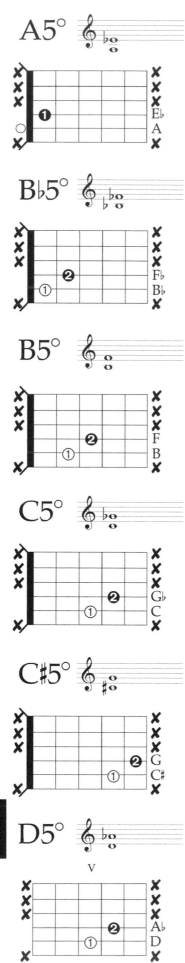

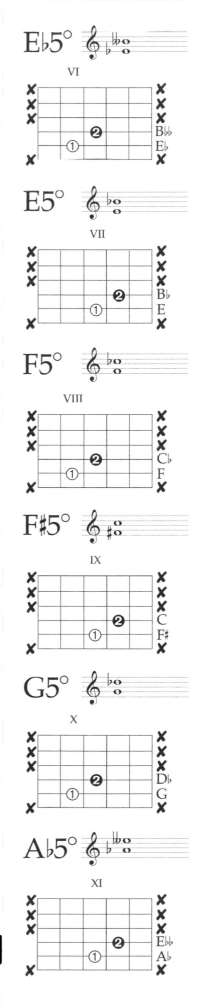

E♭5° VI — B♭♭, E♭

E5° VII — B♭, E

F5° VIII — C♭, F

F♯5° IX — C, F♯

G5° X — D♭, G

A♭5° XI — E♭♭, A♭

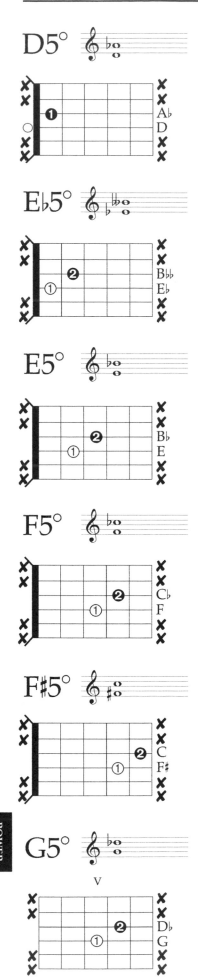

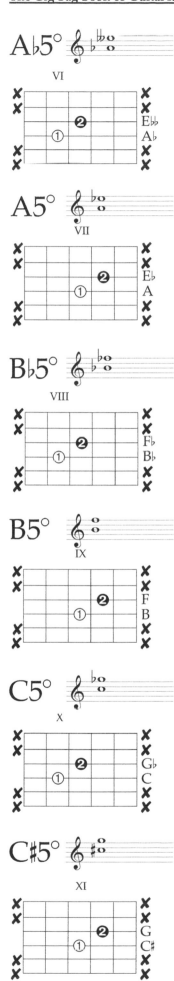

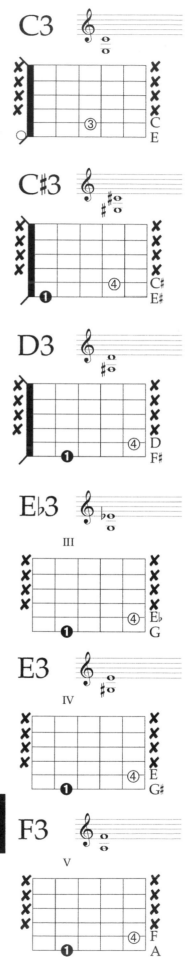

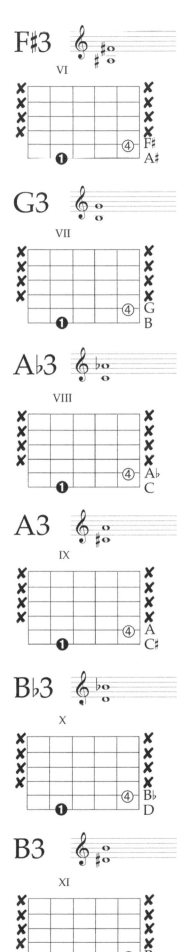

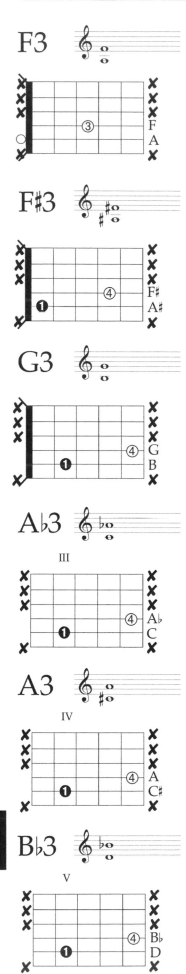

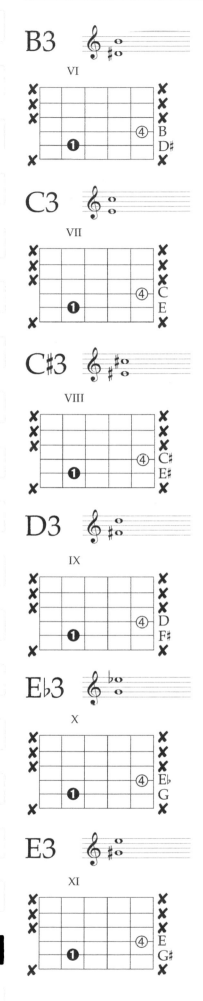

B♭3

B3

C3

C♯3

III

D3

IV

E♭3

V

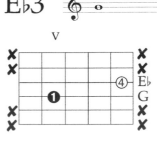

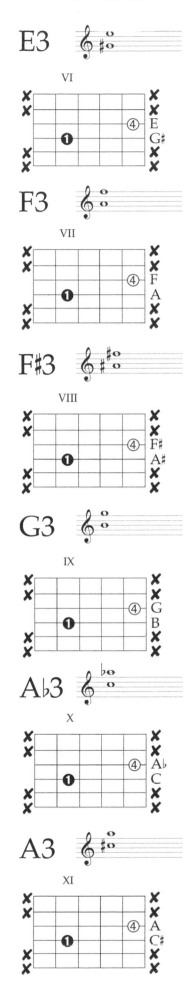

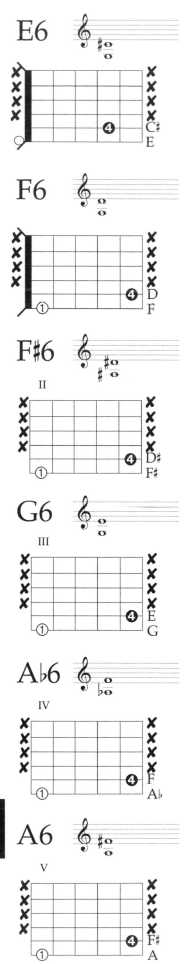

E6

F6

F#6

G6

A♭6

A6

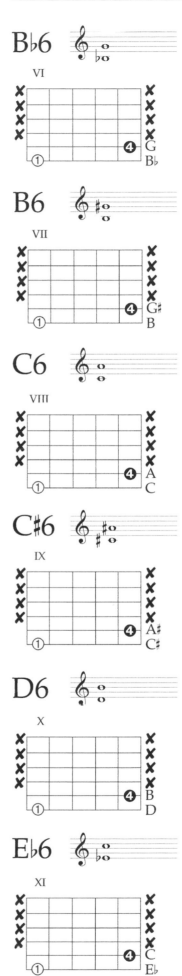

Bb6

B6

C6

C#6

D6

Eb6

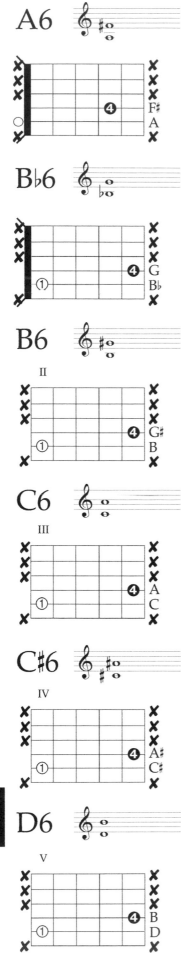

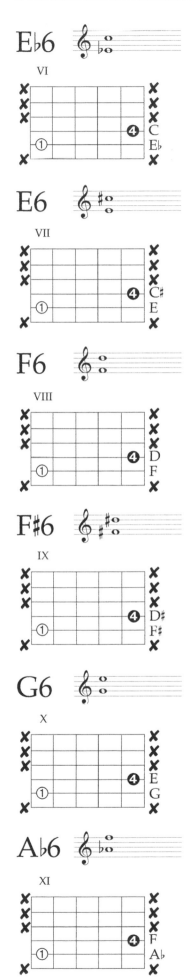

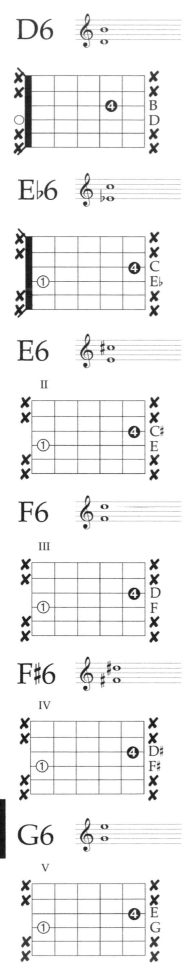

D6

Eb6

E6
II

F6
III

F#6
IV

G6
V

Ab6

A6

Bb6

B6

C6

C#6

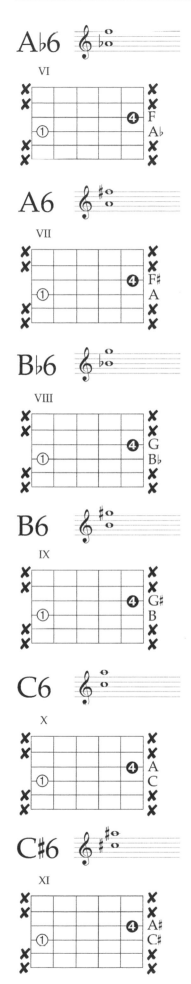

C / C

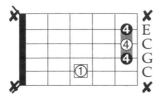

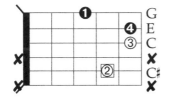

C / C#

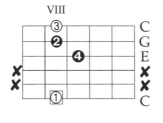

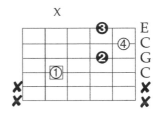

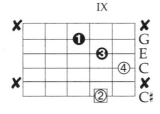

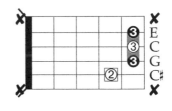

C / D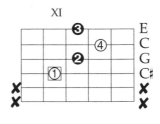

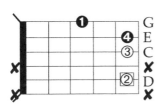

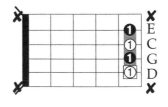

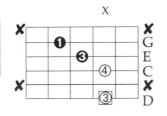

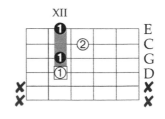

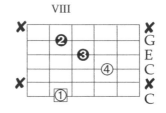

C/Eb

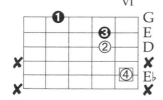
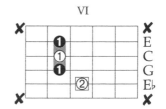
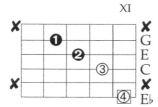
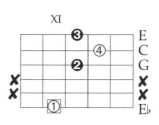

C/E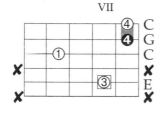
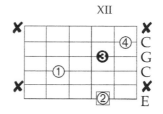
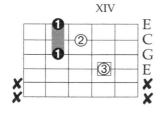

C/F
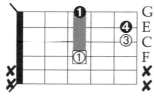
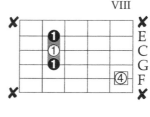
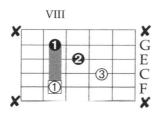
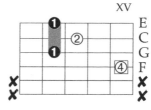

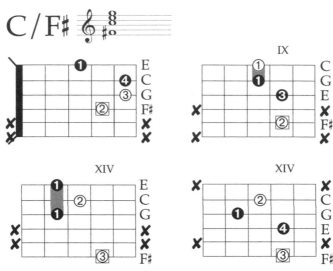

C / F♯

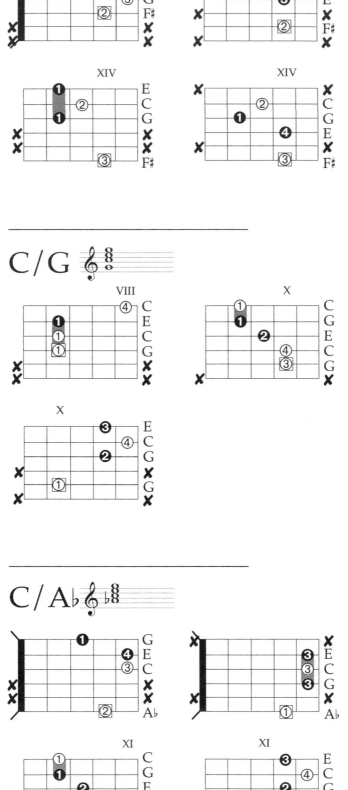

C / G

C / A♭

SLASH
CHORDS

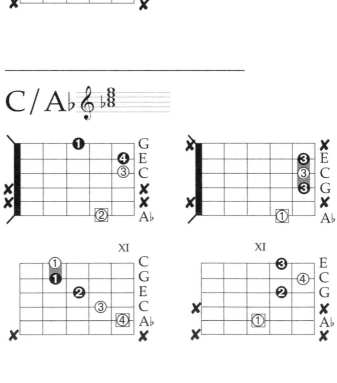

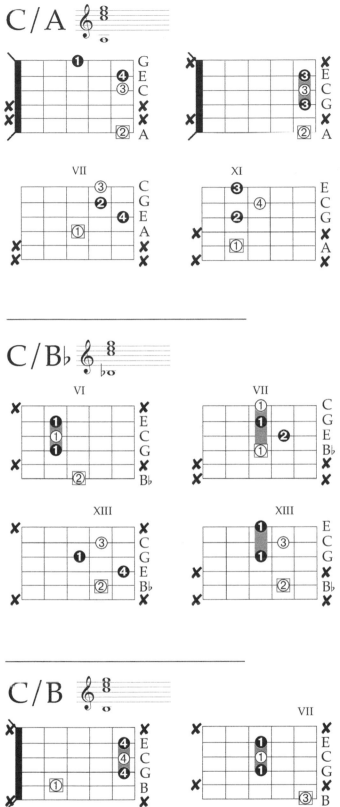

C/A

C/Bb

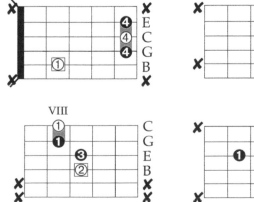

C/B

Transposing

Transposing is the process of rewriting a melody, chord or piece of music into a different key. The relative note intervals remain the same. Unlike the piano, where transposing a chord to a different key results in different finger positions, the guitarist keeps the same finger positions and merely moves up or down the fretboard. As an example, we'll take a look at the F major bar chord. As you can see, to transpose this chord to F♯ major it is simply a matter of moving up a half-step, or one fret position. To further transpose to a G major chord, the F♯ major chord is moved up one fret position.

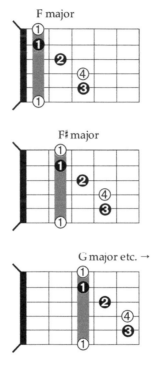

F major

F♯ major

G major etc. →

Not all the possible chords on the guitar reflect this simple relationship - this is particularly not true for chords in the first five frets of the instrument where it becomes necessary to alter the fingering. However, as you become more familiar with this book, you will notice that the majority of chords can be transposed in this manner.